F Journey with the ATHERS

The Word of God Throughout the Ages

New Testament

3

F Journey with the ATHERS

Commentaries on the Sunday Gospels

Year C

edited by
Edith Barnecut, O.S.B.

foreword by
John E. Rotelle, O.S.A.

New City Press

Published in the United States by New City Press
202 Cardinal Rd., Hyde Park, NY 12538
©1994 New City Press

Readings and biographical sketches
©1981, 1984 Friends of Henry Ashworth.

Library of Congress Cataloging-in-Publication Data:

Journey with the Fathers

    (the word of God throughout the ages.   New Testament)
    Includes bibliographical references and indexes.
    Contents: [1] Year A — [2] Year B — [3] Year C.
    1. Church year—Prayer-books and devotions—English.
  2. Bible. N.T. Gospels—Commentaries   3. Fathers
  of the church.   I. Barnecut, Edith.
  BX2178.J68   1992   264'.34   92-20685
  ISBN 1-56548-013-9 (v. 1)
  ISBN 1-56548-056-2 (v. 2)
  ISBN 1-56548-064-3 (v. 3)

Printed in the United States of America

Contents

Editor's Note

This collection of homilies on the Sunday gospels and principal feasts which replace the Sunday celebration is largely a revision of that first published for the Benedictine Office of Vigils. Texts drawn from the patristic period, supplemented by some from later writers following the same tradition, are now offered to a wider public in a fresh format.

Foreword

Throughout the Christian centuries the Bible, especially the gospels, has inspired many volumes of sermons and commentaries. Those written in the early ages of the Church have a special value because of their formative influence on later theology and spirituality—the two were always wedded. It was for this reason that some of the early Christian writers came to be known as the "Fathers of the Church."

The esteem in which these early writings were held is shown by the great labor that was undertaken to copy them by hand so that they became familiar to scholars throughout the known world. Sermons preached by Saint Augustine of Hippo in North Africa in the fifth century were read by Saint Bede in England in the eighth.

Meanwhile translations were being made, though these were mostly of the theological and philosophical works of the Fathers or Church writers, the sermons receiving less attention. Not all of these writings, even of the sermons, speak to people of our day. Many are too diffuse for modern taste, or deal with subjects which are no longer of current interest. To find the gems concealed in this huge mass of material requires great labor, but this was undertaken after the Second Vatican Council to produce the readings in the revised Liturgy of the Hours published in 1970 and later translated into the various languages. This put the choicest passages from our patristic heritage within reach of the general reader. It was quickly supplemented by other collections of patristic and modern readings, one such being the present series *Journey with the Fathers* which will deepen one's understanding of the gospels read at Mass on Sundays or feasts which replace a Sunday. It puts within reach of all some of the treasures of our Christian tradition.

John E. Rotelle, O.S.A.

First Sunday of Advent

Gospel: Luke 21:25-28.34-36

Your redemption is near at hand.

Commentary: Gregory the Great

The Lord says, *Heaven and earth will pass away, but my words will not pass away.* He means: "Nothing that is lasting in your world lasts for eternity without change; and everything that in me is perceived as passing away is kept firm, without passing away. My utterance, which passes away, expresses thoughts that endure without change."

My friends, what we have heard is now clear. Daily the world is oppressed by new and growing evils. You see how few of you remain from a countless people; yet daily afflictions still oppress us, sudden disasters crush us, new and unforeseen misfortunes afflict us. In youth the body is vigorous, the chest remains strong and healthy, the neck is straight, the arms muscular; in later years the body is bent, the neck scrawny and withered, the chest oppressed by difficult breathing, strength is failing, and speech is interrupted by wheezing. Weakness may not yet be present, but often in the case of the senses their healthy state is itself a malady. So too the world was strong in its early years, as in its youth: lusty in begetting offspring for the human race, green in its physical health, teeming with a wealth of resources. Now it is weighed down by its old age, and as troubles increase it is oppressed as if by the proximity of its demise.

Therefore, my friends, do not love what you see cannot long exist. Keep in mind the apostle's precept, in which he counsels us *not to love the world or the things in the world, because if anyone loves the world the love of the Father is not in him.* The day before yesterday, my friends, you heard that an old orchard was uprooted by a sudden hurricane, that homes were destroyed and churches knocked from their foundations. How many persons who were safe and unharmed in the evening, thinking of what they would do the next day, suddenly died that night, caught in a trap of destruction?

We must reflect that to bring these things about our unseen Judge caused the movement of a very slight breeze; he called a storm out of a single cloud and overthrew the earth, he struck the foundations of many buildings, causing them to fall. What will that Judge do when he comes in person, when his anger is burning to punish sinners, if we cannot bear him when he strikes us with an insignificant cloud? What flesh will withstand the presence of his anger, if he moved the wind and overthrew the earth, stirred up the air and destroyed so many buildings? Paul referred to this severity of the Judge who is to come and said: *It is a fearful thing to fall into the hands of the living God.*

Dearly beloved, keep that day before your eyes, and whatever you now believe to be burdensome will be light in comparison with it. The Lord says of this day through the prophet: *Yet once more and I will shake not only the earth but also the heavens.*

You see how he moved the air, as I said, and the earth did not withstand it. Who then will bear it when he moves the sky? What shall we call these terrors we see but heralds of the wrath to come? We must reflect that these troubles are as much unlike the final one as the herald's role is unlike the judge's power. Give hard thought to that day, dearly beloved; amend your lives, change your habits, resist and overcome your evil temptations. The more you now anticipate his severity by fear, the more securely will you behold the coming of your eternal Judge.

(Forty Gospel Homilies: PL 76, 1077)

Gregory the Great (c.540-604), a Roman by birth, is one of the four great doctors of the Western Church. His great grandfather was Pope Felix III (483-492). After a brilliant secular career he became a monk, having turned his own house on the Clivus Scauri into a monastery dedicated to Saint Andrew. From c.578 to 585 he was in Constantinople as "apocrisiarius," or papal nuncio, at the imperial court. His *Morals on Job* were conferences given at their request to the small band of monks who accompanied him there. On 3 September 590 he was elevated to the see of Peter in succession to Pelagius II. Apart from Saint Leo the Great, Gregory is the only pope who has left examples of his preaching to the Roman people. These are his homilies on the gospels, and on Ezekiel. His *Book of Pastoral Rule* became the textbook of medieval bishops. Gregory is known as the apostle of the English because he sent the monk, Saint Augustine of Canterbury, to evangelize England.

Second Sunday of Advent

Gospel: Luke 3:1-6

All humankind shall see the salvation of God.

Commentary: Origen of Alexandria

The word of God was addressed to John, son of Zechariah, in the desert, and he went through all the Jordan valley. Where else could he go but through the Jordan valley, where there would be water at hand to baptize those wishing to amend their lives?

Now the word Jordan means descent or coming down. Coming down and rushing in full flood is the river of God, the Lord our Savior, in whom we were baptized. This is the real, life-giving water, and the sins of those baptized in it are forgiven.

So come, catechumens, and amend your lives so that you may have your sins forgiven in baptism. In baptism the sins of those who cease to sin are forgiven, but if anyone comes to be baptized while continuing to sin, that person's sins are not forgiven. This is why I urge you not to present yourselves for baptism without thinking very carefully, but to give some evidence that you really mean to change your way of living. Spend some time living a good life. Cleanse yourselves from all impurity and avoid every sin. Then, when you yourselves have begun to despise your sins, they will be forgiven you. You will be forgiven your sins if you renounce them.

The teaching of the Old Testament is the same. We read in the prophet Isaiah: *A voice cries out in the desert: Prepare a way for the Lord. Build him a straight highway.* What way shall we prepare for the Lord? A way by land? Could the Word of God travel such a road? Is it not rather a way within ourselves that we have to prepare for the Lord? Is it not a straight and level highway in our hearts that we are to make ready? Surely this is the way by which the Word of God enters, a way that exists in the spaciousness of the human body. The human heart is vast, broad, and capacious, if only it is pure. Would you like to know its length and breadth? See then what a vast amount of divine knowledge it can contain.

Solomon says: *He gave me knowledge of all that exists; he taught me about the structure of the universe and the properties of the elements, the beginning and the end of epochs and the periods between, the variations in the seasons and the succession of the months, the revolution of the year and the position of the stars, the nature of living things and the instincts of wild animals, the force of the winds and the thoughts of human beings, the various kinds of plants and the medicinal properties of roots.*

You must realize that the human heart is not small when it can contain all this. You ought to judge it not by its physical size but by its power to embrace such a vast amount of knowledge of the truth.

But so that I may convince you that the human heart is large by a simple example from daily life, let us consider this. Whatever city we may have passed through, we have in our minds. We remember its streets, walls, and buildings, what they were like and where they were situated. We have a mental picture of the roads we have traveled. In moments of quiet reflection our minds embrace the sea that we have crossed. So, as I said, the heart that can contain all this is not small!

Therefore, if what contains so much is not small, let a way be prepared in it for the Lord, a straight highway along which the Word and Wisdom of God may advance. Prepare a way for the Lord by living a good life and guard that way by good works. Let the Word of God move in you unhindered and give you a knowledge of his coming and of his mysteries. To him be glory and power for ever and ever. Amen.

(On Luke's Gospel 21: PG 13, 1855-1856)

Origen (183-253), one of the greatest thinkers of ancient times, became head of the catechetical school of Alexandria at the age of eighteen. In 230 he was ordained priest by the bishop of Caesarea. His life was entirely devoted to the study of scripture and he was also a great master of the spiritual life. His book *On First Principles* was the first great theological synthesis. Many of his works are extant only in Latin as a result of his posthumous condemnation for heterodox teaching. Nevertheless, in intention he was always a loyal son of the Church.

Third Sunday of Advent

Gospel: Luke 3:10-18

What must we do?

Commentary: Origen of Alexandria

The baptism that Jesus gives is a baptism in the Holy Spirit and in fire. Baptism is one and the same no matter who receives it, but its effect depends on the recipient's disposition. He who is portrayed as baptizing in the Holy Spirit and in fire *holds a winnowing fan in his hand, which he will use to clear his threshing floor. The wheat he will gather into his barn, but the chaff he will burn with fire that can never be quenched.*

I should like to discover our Lord's reason for holding a winnowing fan and to inquire into the nature of the wind that scatters the light chaff here and there, leaving the heavier grain lying in a heap—for you must have a wind if you want to separate wheat and chaff.

I suggest that the faithful are like a heap of unsifted grain, and that the wind represents the temptations which assail them and show up the wheat and the chaff among them. When your soul is overcome by some temptation, it is not the temptation that turns you into chaff. No, you were chaff already, that is to say fickle and faithless; the temptation simply discloses the stuff you are made of. On the other hand, when you endure temptations bravely it is not the temptation that makes you faithful and patient; temptation merely brings to light the hidden virtues of patience and fortitude that have been present in you all along. *Do you think I had any other purpose in speaking to you,* said the Lord to Job, *than to reveal your virtue?* In another text he declares: *I humbled you and made you feel the pangs of hunger in order to find out what was in your heart.*

In the same way, a storm will not allow a house to stand firm if it is built upon sand. If you wish to build a house, you must build it upon rock. Then any storms that arise will not demolish your handiwork, whereas the house built upon sand will totter, proving thereby that it is not well founded.

So while all is yet quiet, before the storm gathers, before the squalls begin to bluster or the waves to swell, let us concentrate all our efforts on the foundations of our building and construct our house with the many strong, interlocking bricks of God's commandments. Then when cruel persecution is unleashed like some fearful tornado against Christians, we shall be able to show that our house is built upon Christ Jesus our rock.

Far be it from us to deny Christ when that time comes. But if anyone should do so, let that person realize that it was not at the moment of his public denial that his apostasy took place. Its seeds and roots had been hidden within him for a long time; persecution only brought into the open and made public what was already there. Let us pray to the Lord then that we may be firm and solid buildings that no storm can overthrow, founded on the rock of our Lord Jesus Christ, to whom be glory and power for ever and ever. Amen.

(On Luke's Gospel 26, 3-5: SC 87, 340-342)

Origen (183-253), one of the greatest thinkers of ancient times, became head of the catechetical school of Alexandria at the age of eighteen. In 230 he was ordained priest by the bishop of Caesarea. His life was entirely devoted to the study of scripture and he was also a great master of the spiritual life. His book *On First Principles* was the first great theological synthesis. Many of his works are extant only in Latin as a result of his posthumous condemnation for heterodox teaching. Nevertheless, in intention he was always a loyal son of the Church.

Fourth Sunday of Advent

Gospel: Luke 1:39-45

Why should I be honored with a visit from the mother of my Lord?

Commentary: Guerric of Igny

Our King and Savior is coming; let us run to meet him! *Good news from a far country,* in the words of Solomon, *is like cold water to a thirsty soul;* and to announce the coming of our Savior and the reconciliation of the world, together with the good things of the life to come, is to bring good news indeed. *How beautiful are the feet of those who bring good tidings and publish peace!* Such messengers truly bear a refreshing draught to the soul that thirsts for God; with their news of the Savior's coming, they joyfully draw and offer us water from the springs of salvation. In the words and spirit of Elizabeth, the soul responds to the message, whether it be of Isaiah or of his fellow-prophets: *Why is this granted to me, that my Lord should come to me? For behold, when the voice of your greeting came to my ears,* my spirit leapt for joy within me in eager longing to run ahead to meet my God and Savior.

Let us too arise with joy and run in spirit to meet our Savior. Hailing him from afar, let us worship him, saying: Come, Lord, *save me and I shall be saved!* Come and *show us your face, and we shall all be saved. We have been waiting for you; be our help in time of trouble.* This was how the prophets and saints of old ran to meet the Messiah, filled with immense desire to see with their eyes, if possible, what they already saw in spirit.

We must look forward to the day, so soon to come, on which we celebrate the anniversary of Christ's birth. Scripture itself insists on the joy which must fill us—a joy which will lift our spirit out of itself in longing for his coming, impatient of delay as it strains forward to see even now what the future holds in store.

I believe that the many texts of scripture which urge us to go out to meet him speak of Christ's first coming as well as his second. This may raise a query in your mind. Surely, however, we are to understand that as our bodies will rise up rejoicing at his second coming, so our hearts must run forward in joy to greet his first.

Between these two comings of his, the Lord frequently visits us individually in accordance with our merits and desires, forming us to the likeness of his first coming in the flesh, and preparing us for his return at the end of time. He comes to us now, to make sure that we do not lose the fruits of his first coming nor incur his wrath at his second. His purpose now is to convert our pride into the humility which he showed when he first came, so that he may refashion our lowly bodies into the likeness of that glorious body which he will manifest when he comes again.

Grace accompanied his first coming, glory will surround his last; this intermediate coming is a combination of both, enabling us to experience in the consolations of his grace a sort of foretaste of his glory. Blessed are those whose burning love has gained for them such a privilege!

And so, my brothers, though we have not yet experienced this wonderful consolation, we are encouraged by firm faith and a pure conscience to wait patiently for the Lord to come. In joy and confidence let us say with Saint Paul: *I know the one in whom I have put my trust, and I am confident of his power to guard what has been put into my charge until the day when our great God and Savior Jesus Christ comes in glory.* May he be praised for ever and ever! Amen

(Second Sermon for Advent 1-4: SC 166, 104-116)

Guerric of Igny (c.1070/1080-1157), about whose early life little is known, probably received his education at the cathedral school of Tournai, perhaps under the influence of Odo of Cambrai (1807-1092). He seems to have lived a retired life of prayer and study near the cathedral of Tournai. He paid a visit to Clairvaux to consult Saint Bernard, and is mentioned by him as a novice in a letter to Ogerius in 1125/1256. He became abbot of the Cistercian abbey of Igny, in the diocese of Rheims in 1138. A collection of 54 authentic sermons preached on Sundays and feast days has been edited. Guerric's spirituality was influenced by Origen.

Christmas

Gospel: John 1:1-18

The Word was made flesh, he lived among us, and we saw his glory.

Commentary: Julian of Vezalay

W*hile everything was hushed and still, and night was half way through its course, your almighty Word, O Lord, leaped down from your royal throne in the heavens.* In this text of scripture, written long before, the most sacred moment of all time is made known to us, the moment when God's almighty Word would leave his Father's tender embrace and come down into his mother's womb to bring us his message of salvation. *For God, who in many and various ways in the past spoke to our fathers through the prophets, in these last days has spoken to us through his Son,* declaring: *This is my beloved Son in whom I am well pleased; listen to him.* And so from his royal throne the Word of God came to us, humbling himself in order to raise us up, becoming poor to make us rich, and human to make us divine.

But the people he was to redeem needed to have great trust and hope that the word would come to them with effective power. Hence the description of God's Word as almighty: *Your almighty Word* the Bible calls him. So lost, so wholly abandoned to unhappiness was the human race, that it could only trust in a word that was almighty; otherwise it would experience no more than a weak and tremulous hope of being set free from sin and its effects. To give poor lost humanity an absolute assurance of being saved, the Word that came to save it was therefore called almighty.

And see how truly almighty was that Word. When *neither heaven nor anything under the heavens as yet had any existence, he spoke and they came into being,* made out of nothing. The almighty power of the Word created substance and shape simultaneously. At his command, "Let there be a world," the world came into being, and when he decreed, "Let there be human beings," human beings were created.

18

But the Word of God did not remake his creatures as easily as he made them. He made them by simply giving a command; he remade them by dying. He made them by commanding; he remade them by suffering. "You have burdened me," he told them, "with your sinning. To direct and govern the whole fabric of the world is no effort for me, for *I have power to reach from one end of the earth to the other and to order all things as I please.* It is only human beings, with their obstinate disregard for the law I laid down for them who have caused me distress by their sins. That is why I came down from my royal throne, why I did not shrink from enclosing myself in the Virgin's womb nor from entering into a personal union with poor lost humanity. A newborn babe in swaddling bands, I lay in a manger, since the Creator of the world could find no room at the inn."

And so there came a deep silence. Everything was still. The voices of prophets and apostles were hushed, since the prophets had already delivered their message, while the time for the apostles' preaching had yet to come. Between these two proclamations a period of silence intervened, and in the midst of this silence the Father's almighty Word leaped down from his royal throne. There is a beautiful fitness here: in the intervening silence the mediator between God and the human race also intervened, coming as a human being to human beings, as a mortal to mortals, to save the dead from death.

I pray that the Word of the Lord may come again today to those who are silent, and that we may hear what the Lord God says to us in our hearts. Let us silence the desires and importunings of the flesh and the vainglorious fantasies of our imagination, so that we can freely hear what the Spirit is saying; for the Spirit is always speaking to us, but as long as we fix our attention upon other things, we fail to hear what the Spirit is saying.

(Sermon 1 on Christmas: SC 192, 45.52.60)

Julian of Vezalay (1080-1160) was a Benedictine monk who, in the later years of his life, was given responsibility for the spiritual life of his community. His famous sermons, twenty-seven of which were published, show a knowledge of Latin classics and Greek philosophy, especially that of Plato, a strong attachment to patristic traditions, and a discrete use of allegory.

Holy Family

Gospel: Luke 2:41-52

His parents found Jesus in the temple, sitting among the doctors, listening to them.

Commentary: Origen of Alexandria

When Jesus was twelve years old, he stayed behind in Jerusalem. Not knowing this, his parents sought him anxiously, but did not find him. Though they searched the whole caravan, looking for him among their kinsfolk and acquaintances, he was nowhere to be found.

It was his own parents who were looking for him—the father who had brought him up and cared for him when they fled into Egypt—and even they did not find him at once. This shows that Jesus is not found among relatives and acquaintances, nor among those bound to him by physical ties. We do not find him in a crowd. Let us learn where it was that Joseph and Mary discovered him; then in their company we too shall be able to find him.

They found him, scripture says, in the temple. Not just anywhere, but in the temple; and not just anywhere in the temple, but among the doctors, listening to them and asking them questions. And so we too must look for Jesus in the temple of God; we must look for him in the Church, among the doctors who belong to the Church and are faithful to its teaching. If we seek him there, we shall find him. Moreover, anyone who claims to be a doctor without possessing Christ is a doctor in name only; Jesus, the Word and Wisdom of God, will not be found with him.

They found him, then, *sitting among the doctors*, or rather not merely sitting, but learning from them and listening to them. At this very moment Jesus is present among us too, questioning us and listening to us speaking. It is further written, *And they were all amazed.* What caused their astonishment? Not his questions—though these were certainly extraordinary—but his answers. He questioned the doctors, and since they could not always give an answer, he himself replied to his own questions. These replies were not mere disputation, but real teaching, exemplified for us in holy scripture where the divine law declares: *Moses spoke, and God answered him.* In this way the Lord instructed Moses about those matters of which he was ignorant. So it was that sometimes Jesus asked questions, sometimes he answered them; and, as we have already said, wonderful though his questions were, his replies were even more wonderful.

In order, therefore, that we too may be his hearers and that he may put to us questions which he himself will then answer, let us pray to him earnestly, seeking him with great effort and anguish, and then our search will be rewarded. Not for nothing was it written: *Your father and I have been looking for you anxiously.* The search for Jesus must be neither careless nor indifferent, nor must it be only a transitory affair. Those who seek in this manner will never find him. We must truly be able to say: *We have been looking for you anxiously;* if we can say this then he will reply to our weary and anxious soul in the words: *Did you not know that I must be in my Father's house?*

(On Luke's Gospel 18, 2-5: GCS 9, 112-113)

Origen (183-253), one of the greatest thinkers of ancient times, became head of the catechetical school of Alexandria at the age of eighteen. In 230 he was ordained priest by the bishop of Caesarea. His life was entirely devoted to the study of scripture and he was also a great master of the spiritual life. His book *On First Principles* was the first great theological synthesis. Many of his works are extant only in Latin as a result of his posthumous condemnation for heterodox teaching. Nevertheless, in intention he was always a loyal son of the Church.

Mary, Mother of God

Gospel: Luke 2:16-21

The shepherds found Mary and Joseph, and the infant lying in the crib.

Commentary: Basil of Seleucia

Born of the Virgin Mother of God, the Creator and Lord of all shared our human nature, for he had a real body and soul even though he had no part in our misdeeds. *He committed no sin,* says scripture, *and no falsehood ever came from his mouth.* O holy womb in which God was received, in which the record of our sins was effaced, in which God became man while remaining God! He was carried in the womb, condescending to be born in the same way as we are. Yet when he was received into the arms of his mother he did not leave the bosom of his Father. God is not divided as he carries out his will, but saves the world without suffering any division in himself. When Gabriel came into the presence of the virgin Mother of God he left heaven behind, but when the Word of God who fills all creation took flesh within her, he was not separated from the adoring hosts of heaven.

Is there any need to enumerate all the prophecies foretelling Christ's birth of the Mother of God? What tongue could worthily hymn her through whom we have received such magnificent blessings? With what flowers of praise could we weave a fitting crown for her from whom sprang the flower of Jesse, who has crowned our race with glory and honor? What gifts could we bring that would be worthy of her of whom the whole world is unworthy? If Paul could say of the other saints that the world was not worthy of them, what can we say of the Mother of God, who outshines all the martyrs even as the sun outshines the stars? O Virgin, well may the angels rejoice in you! Because of you they who long ages ago had banished our race are now sent to our service, and to his joy Gabriel is entrusted with the news of a divine child's conception. *Rejoice, most favored one,* let your face glow with gladness. You are to give birth to the joy of all the world, who will put an end to the age-old curse, destroying the power of death and giving to all the hope of resurrection.

Emmanuel came into the world he had made long before. God from all eternity, he came as a newborn infant. He who had prepared eternal dwellings lay in a manger, for there was no room for him at the inn. He who was made known by a star came to birth in a cave. He who was offered as a ransom for sin received gifts from the wise men. He who as God enfolds the whole world in his embrace was taken into the arms of Simeon. The shepherds gazed upon this baby; the angelic host, knowing he was God, sang of his glory in heaven and of peace to his people on earth. And all these things together with other marvels concerning him, the holy mother of the Lord of all creation, the mother in very truth of God, *pondered in her heart,* and her heart was filled with great gladness. She was radiant with joy and amazed when she thought of the majesty of her Son who was also God. As her gaze rested upon that divine child I think she must have been overwhelmed by awe and longing. She was alone conversing with the Alone.

(Homily 39, 4.5: PG 85, 438.442.446)

Basil of Seleucia (c.459) became archbishop of Seleucia about the year 440. He is remembered for his fluctuating attitude in the events which preceded the Council of Chalcedon in 451. He voted against Monophysitism at the Synod of Constantinople in 448, but at the "Robber Synod" of Ephesus in 449 gave his support to Eutyches, the originator of Monophysitism. Then at the Council of Chalcedon he signed the Tome of Saint Leo, which condemned Eutyches. Thirty-nine of Basil's homilies have been preserved. They show his concern to place the exegesis of his time within the reach of all.

Second Sunday after Christmas

Gospel: John 1:1-18

The Word was made flesh, he lived among us, and we saw his glory.

Commentary: Basil the Great

God is on earth, God is among us, not now as lawgiver—there is no fire, trumpet blast, smoke-wreathed mountain, dense cloud, or storm to terrify whoever hears him—but as one gently and kindly conversing in a human body with his fellow men and women. God is in the flesh. Now he is not acting intermittently as he did through the prophets. He is bringing back to himself the whole human race, which he has taken possession of and united to himself. By his flesh he has made the human race his own kin.

But how can glory come to all through only one? How can the Godhead be in the flesh? In the same way as fire can be in iron: not by moving from place to place but by the one imparting to the other its own properties. Fire does not speed toward iron, but without itself undergoing any change it causes the iron to share in its own natural attributes. The fire is not diminished and yet it completely fills whatever shares in its nature. So is it also with God the Word. He did not relinquish his own nature and yet *he dwelt among us.* He did not undergo any change and yet *the Word became flesh.* Earth received him from heaven, yet heaven was not deserted by him who holds the universe in being.

Let us strive to comprehend the mystery. The reason God is in the flesh is to kill the death that lurks there. As diseases are cured by medicines assimilated by the body, and as darkness in a house is dispelled by the coming of light, so death, which held sway over human nature, is done away with by the coming of God. And as ice formed on water covers its surface as long as night and darkness last but melts under the warmth of the sun, so death reigned until the

24

coming of Christ; but when the grace of God our Savior appeared and the Sun of Justice rose, death was swallowed up in victory, unable to bear the presence of true life. How great is God's goodness, how deep his love for us!

Let us join the shepherds in giving glory to God, let us dance with the angels and sing: *Today a savior has been born to us. He is Christ the Lord. The Lord is God and he has appeared to us,* not as God, which would have been terrifying for our weakness, but as a slave so as to free those who live in slavery. Who could be so lacking in sensibility and so ungrateful as not to join all here present in our gladness, exultation, and radiant joy? This feast belongs to the whole of creation. Let everyone contribute and be grateful. Let our voices too ring out in songs of jubilation.

(Homily on Christ's Ancestry 2.6: PG 31, 1459-1462.1471-1474)

Basil the Great (c.330-379), one of the three great Cappadocian Fathers, received an excellent education and began a career as a rhetorician before a spiritual awakening led him to receive baptism and become a monk. After visiting ascetics in Egypt, Palestine, Syria, and Mesopotamia, he decided that it was better for monks to live together in monasteries than alone as hermits, and he set about organizing Cappadocian monasticism. Basil's Rules influenced Saint Benedict. In 370 Basil succeeded Eusebius as bishop of Caesarea. His main concern was for the unity of the Church, and he strove to establish better relations between Rome and the East. His efforts bore fruit only after his death. Basil's writings include dogmatic, ascetic, and pedagogic treatises as well as letters and sermons.

Epiphany

Gospel: Matthew 2:1-12

We have come from the east to worship the king.

Commentary: Odilo of Cluny

This is the day on which Christ was clearly revealed to the world, the day on which he consecrated the sacrament of baptism by receiving it in person, and also the day, according to the belief of the faithful, on which he changed water into wine at the wedding feast. On this day too water became wine in a spiritual sense; the letter of the law ceased to apply, and the grace of the gospel shone out through Christ.

Christ was baptized, and the world was renewed. At his baptism the world put off the old man and put on the new. The earth cast off the first man who is earthly by nature and put on the second man who comes from heaven. When Christ was baptized the mystery of holy baptism was consecrated by the presence of the whole Trinity. The Father's voice thundered: *This my beloved Son in whom I am well pleased.* The Holy Spirit appeared in the form of a dove. But it was the divine will that only the Son should be baptized by blessed John. Although the whole Trinity was at work in the incarnation of the Word and the mystery of his baptism, the Son alone was baptized by John, just as he alone was born of the Virgin. With the exception of sin, he experienced all the sufferings of the humanity he had assumed, yet in his divinity he remained untouched by suffering.

Today is festive enough in its own right, but it stands out all the more clearly because of its proximity to Christmas. When God is worshiped in the Child, the honor of the virgin birth is revered. When gifts are brought to the God-man, the dignity of the divine motherhood is exalted. When Mary is found with her child, Christ's true manhood is proclaimed, together with the inviolate chastity of the Mother of

God. All this is contained in the evangelist's statement: *And entering the house they found the child with Mary his mother, and bowing down they worshiped him. Then, opening their treasures, they offered him gifts: gold, frankincense, and myrrh.*

The gifts brought by the wise men reveal hidden mysteries concerning Christ. To offer gold is to proclaim his kingship, to offer incense is to adore his godhead, and to offer myrrh is to acknowledge his mortality. We too must have faith in Christ's assumption of our mortal nature. Then we shall realize that our two-fold death has been abrogated by the death he died once for all. You will find a description in Isaiah of how Christ appeared as a mortal man and freed us from our debt to death. It is written: *He was led like a lamb to the slaughter.*

The necessity of faith in the kingship of Christ can be demonstrated on divine authority, since he says of himself in one of the psalms: *I have been appointed king by him,* that is, by God the Father. And speaking as Wisdom personified he claims to be the King of kings, saying: *It is through me that kings reign and princes pronounce judgment.*

As to Christ's divinity, the whole world created by him testifies that he is the Lord. He himself says in the gospel: *All power has been given me in heaven and on earth,* and the blessed evangelist declares: *All things were made through him, and without him nothing was made.*

(Sermon 2 on the Epiphany: PL 142, 997-998)

Odilo (962-1049) entered the monastery of Cluny in 991 and a few years later was elected abbot, a position he held for fifty years. Under his rule the number of Cluniac houses increased from thirty-seven to sixty-five and their influence was widespread. Odilo left a lasting mark on the liturgy by introducing the commemoration of the dead on All Souls' day. From Cluny this observance spread throughout the Western Church. Odilo wrote a number of letters and sermons, most of which treat of the Blessed Virgin and the mysteries of redemption, especially the incarnation.

Baptism of the Lord

Gospel: Luke 3:15-16.21-22

Someone is coming who is more powerful than I am; he will baptize you with the
Holy Spirit and with fire.

Commentary: Attributed to Hippolytus of Rome

As soon as he had been baptized, Jesus came out of the water. The
heavens were opened to him and the Spirit of God in the form of
a dove came down and rested on him. Then a voice from heaven said:
This is my beloved Son in whom I am well pleased.

If the Lord had yielded to John's persuasion and had not been
baptized, do you realize what great blessings and how many we should
have been deprived of? Heaven was closed until then; our homeland
on high was inaccessible. Once we had descended into the depths we
were incapable of rising again to such lofty heights. The Lord was not
only baptized himself; he also renewed our fallen nature and restored
to us our status as God's children. At once *the heavens were opened
to him.* The world we see was reconciled with the world that lies
beyond our vision; the angels were filled with joy; earthly disorders
were remedied; mysteries were revealed; enemies were made friends.

The heavens were opened to him you have heard the evangelist say.
This happened for three wonderful reasons. The heavenly bridal
chamber had to open its shining gates to Christ at his baptism because
he was the bridegroom. The gates of heaven had also to be lifted up
to allow the Holy Spirit to descend in the form of a dove and the
Father's voice to resound far and wide. The heavens were opened to
him and a voice said: *This is my beloved Son in whom I am well
pleased.*

This is my beloved Son who appeared on earth without leaving his
Father's side. He both appeared and did not appear, for he was not
what he seemed. As far as appearance goes the one who confers
baptism is superior to the one who receives it. This is why the Father

sent the Holy Spirit down on him from heaven. As in Noah's ark a dove revealed God's love for the human race, so now it was in the form of a dove, as though with an olive branch in its beak, that the Spirit descended and rested on him to whom the Father would bear witness. He did so to make sure that the Father's voice would be recognized and the ancient prophecy believed. Which prophecy? The one that says: *The Lord's voice resounded over the waters. The God of glory thunders, the Lord thunders across many waters.* And what does he say? *This is my beloved Son in whom I am well pleased.*

Pay close attention now, I beg you, for I want to return to the fountain of life and contemplate its healing waters at their source. The Father of immortality sent his immortal Son and Word into the world; he came to us to cleanse us with water and the Spirit. To give us a new birth that would make our bodies and souls immortal, he breathed into us the Spirit of life and armed us with incorruptibility.

Therefore in a herald's voice I cry: Peoples of every nation, come and receive the immortality given in baptism. To you who have spent all your days in the darkness of ignorance I bring the good news of life. Leave your slavery for freedom, the tyrant's yoke for a kingdom, corruptibility for eternal life. Do you wish to know how to do this? By water and the Holy Spirit. This is to say, by the water through which we are born again and given life, and by the Spirit who is the Comforter sent for your sake to make you a child of God.

(Sermon on the Holy Manifestation 6-9: PG 10, 858-859)

First Sunday of Lent

Gospel: Luke 4:1-13

Jesus was led by the Spirit through the wilderness where he was tempted.

Commentary: John Chrysostom

Then Jesus was led by the Spirit into the desert to be tempted by the devil. What does "then" mean? After the Spirit descended, after the voice from heaven said: *This is my beloved Son in whom I am well pleased.* The amazing thing is that scripture says it was the Holy Spirit who led him there!

All that Jesus did and suffered was for our instruction. He consented to be led into the desert and to do battle with the devil so that when the baptized were assailed by greater temptations after baptism than before they would not be troubled as though this were something unexpected, but would remain steadfast, bearing them all nobly. You did not receive weapons so that you might sit at ease, but so that you might fight!

The reasons God does not prevent the onslaught of temptations are these. First, so that you may learn that you have now become much stronger; then, so that you may remain modest, for you will not be puffed up by the greatness of your gifts if temptations can humble you; next, because the wicked demon may doubt at first whether you have really renounced him and the test of temptation will convince him of your total desertion; fourth, to confirm you, who are now stronger and steadier than iron; fifth, to give you clear evidence of the treasures committed to you. The devil would not have attacked you if he had not seen that you have been raised to a position of great honor.

Notice where it was that the Spirit led Jesus—not into the city or the market place, but into the desert. Since Jesus wished to entice the devil he gave him his opportunity not only by his own hunger, but also by his choice of place. The devil usually attacks people when he sees them alone by themselves. He does not dare to do so when he sees them together with others. It is for this reason especially that we should frequently meet with one another. If we do not we may become an easy prey for the devil. And so, the devil finds Jesus in the desert, in a trackless wilderness.

Consider how vile and wicked the devil's approach is, and what sort of opportunity he watches for. He does not come near when Jesus is fasting, but only when he is hungry. You should learn from this the great value of fasting and that no weapon is more powerful against the devil. After baptism you should not be filled with food and drink from a well-laden table, but should rather devote yourself to fasting. Jesus fasted not because he himself had any need to do so, but to give us an example.

(On Matthew 13, 1: PG 57, 207-209)

John Chrysostom (c.347-407) was born at Antioch and studied under Diodore of Tarsus, the leader of the Antiochene school of theology. After a period of great austerity as a hermit, he returned to Antioch where he was ordained deacon in 381 and priest in 386. From 386 to 397 it was his duty to preach in the principal church of the city, and his best homilies, which earned him the title "Chrysostomos" or "the golden-mouthed," were preached at this time. In 397 Chrysostom became patriarch of Constantinople, where his efforts to reform the court, clergy, and people led to his exile in 404 and finally to his death from the hardships imposed on him. Chrysostom stressed the divinity of Christ against the Arians and his full humanity against the Apollinarians, but he had no speculative bent. He was above all a pastor of souls, and was one of the most attractive personalities of the early Church.

Second Sunday of Lent

Gospel: Luke 9:28-36

As Jesus prayed, the aspect of his face was changed and his clothing became brilliant as lightning.

Commentary: Cyril of Alexandria

With three chosen disciples Jesus went up the mountain. Then he was transfigured by a wonderful light that made even his clothes seem to shine. Moses and Elijah stood by him and spoke with him of how he was going to complete his task on earth by dying in Jerusalem. In other words, they spoke of the mystery of his incarnation, and of his saving passion upon the cross. For the law of Moses and the teaching of the holy prophets clearly foreshadowed the mystery of Christ. The law portrayed it by types and symbols inscribed on tablets. The prophets in many ways foretold that in his own time he would appear, clothed in human nature, and that for the salvation of all our race he would not refuse to suffer death upon the cross.

The presence of Moses and Elijah, and their speaking together, was meant to show unmistakably that the law and the prophets were the attendants of our Lord Jesus Christ. He was their master, whom they had themselves pointed out in advance in prophetic words that proved their perfect harmony with one another. The message of the prophets was in no way at variance with the precepts of the law.

Moses and Elijah did not simply appear in silence; they spoke of how Jesus was to complete his task by dying in Jerusalem, they spoke of his passion and cross, and of the resurrection that would follow. Thinking no doubt that the time for the kingdom of God had already come, Peter would gladly have remained on the mountain. He suggested putting up three tents, hardly knowing what he was saying. But it was not yet time for the end of the world; nor was it in this present time that the hopes of the saints would be fulfilled—those hopes founded on Paul's promise that Christ *would transform our lowly bodies into the likeness of his glorious body.* Only the initial stage of the divine plan had as yet been accomplished. Until its completion was it likely that Christ, who came on earth for love of the world, would give up his wish to die for it? For his submitting to death was the world's salvation, and his resurrection was death's destruction.

As well as the vision of Christ's glory, wonderful beyond all description, something else occurred which was to serve as a vital confirmation, not only of the disciples's faith, but of ours as well. From a cloud on high came the voice of God the Father saying: *This is my beloved Son in whom I am well pleased. Listen to him.*

(Homily 9 on the Transfiguration: PG 77, 1011-1014)

Cyril of Alexandria (d.444) succeeded his uncle Theophilus as patriarch in 412. Until 428 the pen of this brilliant theologian was employed in exegesis and polemics against the Arians; after that date it was devoted almost entirely to refuting the Nestorian heresy. The teaching of Nestorius was condemned in 431 by the Council of Ephesus at which Cyril presided, and Mary's title, Mother of God, was solemnly recognized. The incarnation is central to Cyril's theology. Only if Christ is consubstantial with the Father and with us can he save us, for the meeting ground between God and ourselves is the flesh of Christ. Through our kinship with Christ, the Word made flesh, we become children of God, and share in the filial relation of the Son with the Father.

Third Sunday of Lent

Gospel: Luke 13:1-9

Unless you repent, you will all perish as they did.

Commentary: Augustine of Hippo

It is my Father's glory, Christ said, *that you should bear abundant fruit and become my disciples.* But even when we have glorified the Father by bearing much fruit and becoming Christ's disciples, we still have no right to claim the credit for it as though the work were ours alone. The grace to carry out the work had first to come to us from God, and so the glory is his, not ours. That is why Christ is recorded in another place as saying: *Let your light so shine before others that they may see your good works*—and here, lest they be tempted to attribute those good works to themselves, he immediately added: *and may give the glory for them to your heavenly Father.* This, then, is the Father's glory, that we should bear abundant fruit and become Christ's disciples, since it is only through God's mercy in the first place that we can become the disciples of Christ. *We are God's handiwork, created in Christ Jesus for the performance of good works.*

As the Father has loved me, Jesus says, *so I have loved you. Abide in my love.* There we have the source of every good work of ours. How do they come to be ours? Only because faith is active in love. And how could we ever love, unless we ourselves were loved first? In his first letter John the evangelist made this quite clear. *Let us love God,* he wrote, *because he first loved us.* The Father does indeed love us, but he does so in his Son; we glorify the Father by bearing fruit as branches of the vine which is his son and becoming his disciples.

Abide in my love, he says to us. How may we do that? In the words that follow you have your answer. *If you observe what I command you, then you will truly abide in my love.* But is it love that makes us keep the Lord's commandments, or is it the keeping of them that makes us love him? There can be no doubt that love comes first. Anyone devoid of love will lack all incentive to keep the commandments. When, therefore, Christ says to us: *If you keep my commandments, you will abide in my love,* he is telling us that the observance of the commandments is not the source but rather the gauge and touchstone of our love. It is as though he said to us: Do not suppose you are abiding in my love if you are not keeping my commandments, for it is by observing them that you will abide in my love. That is to say, your observance of my commandments is the proof, the outward manifestation, of the fact that you abide in my love.

Let no one, then, who neglects to keep the divine commandments deceive himself by protesting his love for God. It is only to the extent to which we keep the Lord's commandments that we abide in his love; insofar as we fail to keep them we fail to love. Yet even when we do keep God's commandments, it is not something we do in order to make God love us, for unless he loved us first we should not be able to keep them. It is the gift of his grace, a grace which is accessible to the humble of heart, but beyond the reach of the proud.

(Homilies on the Gospel of John 82, 1-4: CCL 36, 532-534)

Augustine (354-430) was born at Thagaste in Africa and received a Christian education, although he was not baptized until 387. In 391 he was ordained priest and in 395 he became coadjutor bishop to Valerius of Hippo, whom he succeeded in 396. Augustine's theology was formulated in the course of his struggle with three heresies: Manicheism, Donatism, and Pelagianism. His writings are voluminous and his influence on subsequent theology immense. He molded the thought of the Middle Ages down to the thirteenth century. Yet he was above all a pastor and a great spiritual writer.

Fourth Sunday of Lent

Gospel: Luke 15:1-3.11-32

Your brother here was dead and has come to life.

Commentary: John Chrysostom

All that God looks for from us is the slightest opening and he forgives a multitude of sins. Let me tell you a parable that will confirm this.

There were two brothers: they divided their father's goods between them and one stayed home, while the other went away to a foreign country, wasted all he had been given, and then could not bear the shame of his poverty. Now the reason I have told you this parable is so that you will understand that even sins committed after baptism can be forgiven if we face up to them. I do not say this to encourage indolence but to save you from despair, which harms us worse than indolence.

The son who went away represents those who fall after baptism. This is clear from the fact that he is called a son, since no one is called a son unless he is baptized. Also, he lived in his father's house and took a share of all his father's goods. Before baptism no one receives the Father's goods or enters upon the inheritance. We can therefore take all this as signifying the state of believers. Furthermore, the wastrel was the brother of the good man, and no one is a brother unless he has been born again through the Spirit.

What does he say after falling into the depths of evil? *I will return to my father.* The reason the father let him go and did not prevent his departure for a foreign land was so that he might learn well by experience what good things are enjoyed by the one who stays at home. For when words would not convince us God often leaves us to learn from the things that happen to us.

When the profligate returned after going to a foreign country and finding out by experience what a great sin it is to leave the father's house, the father did not remember past injuries but welcomed him with open arms. Why? Because he was a father and not a judge. And there were dances and festivities and banquets and the whole house was full of joy and gladness.

Are you asking: "Is this what he gets for his wickedness?" Not for his wickedness, but for his return home; not for sin, but for repentance; not for evil, but for being converted. What is more, when the elder son was angry at this the father gently won him over, saying: *You were always with me, but he was lost and has been found; he was dead and has come back to life.* "When someone who was lost has to be saved," says the father, "it is not the time for passing judgment or making minute inquiries, but only for mercy and forgiveness."

(On Repentance, Homily 1, 3-4: PG 49, 282-283)

John Chrysostom (c.347-407) was born at Antioch and studied under Diodore of Tarsus, the leader of the Antiochene school of theology. After a period of great austerity as a hermit, he returned to Antioch where he was ordained deacon in 381 and priest in 386. From 386 to 397 it was his duty to preach in the principal church of the city, and his best homilies, which earned him the title "Chrysostomos" or "the golden-mouthed," were preached at this time. In 397 Chrysostom became patriarch of Constantinople, where his efforts to reform the court, clergy, and people led to his exile in 404 and finally to his death from the hardships imposed on him. Chrysostom stressed the divinity of Christ against the Arians and his full humanity against the Apollinarians, but he had no speculative bent. He was above all a pastor of souls, and was one of the most attractive personalities of the early Church.

Fifth Sunday of Lent

Gospel: John 8:1-11

Let the one without sin be the first to throw a stone.

Commentary: Augustine of Hippo

The scribes and Pharisees brought to him a woman who had been caught committing adultery. Now the penalty of the law for adultery was stoning. It was, of course, unthinkable that any of the prescriptions of the law could be unjust, so it followed that anyone whose teaching contravened what the law required would lay himself open to the charge of advocating injustice. The Lord's enemies accordingly said to themselves: "He has a reputation for truth and is regarded as a man of great kindness and forbearance, so we must find a pretext for accusing him on the grounds of injustice. Let us confront him with a woman caught committing adultery, and quote the ruling of the law in her regard. If he orders her to be stoned, he will lose his name for clemency; if he tells us to release her, he will not be upholding justice. There is little doubt that he will say she must be freed, in order not to lose the reputation which has made him so popular. That will be our chance to incriminate him and find him guilty of an offense against the law. We shall be able to say: 'You are an enemy of the law! Your answer is not merely an attack on Moses but on God who gave the law to Moses. You have made yourself liable to the death penalty. You and the woman should both be stoned.'" By voicing such opinions the Lord's enemies might be able to inflame popular feeling against him; they might incite the crowds to denounce him and demand his condemnation.

But look at the way our Lord's answer upheld justice without forgoing clemency. He was not caught in the snare his enemies had laid for him; it is they themselves who were caught in it. He did not say the woman should not be stoned, for then it would look as though he were opposing the law. But he had no intention of saying: "Let her be stoned," because he came not to destroy those he found but to seek those who were lost. Mark his reply. It contains justice, clemency, and truth in full measure. *Let the one among you who has never sinned be the first to throw a stone at her.* Let the sinner be punished, yes—but not by sinners. Let the law be carried out, but not by lawbreakers.

This, unquestionably, is the voice of justice, justice that pierced those men like a javelin. Looking into themselves, they realized their guilt, and one by one they all went out. Two remained behind: the miserable woman, and Mercy. The Lord raised his eyes, and with a gentle look he asked her: *Has no one condemned you?* She replied: *No one, sir.* And he said: *Neither will I condemn you.*

What is this Lord? Are you giving approval to immorality? Not at all. Take note of what follows: *Go and sin no more.*

You see then that the Lord does indeed pass sentence, but it is sin he condemns, not people. One who approved of immorality would have said: *"Neither will I condemn you.* Go and live as you please; you can be sure that I will acquit you. However much you sin, I will release you from all penalty, and from the tortures of hell and the underworld." He did not say that. He said: "Neither will I condemn you; you need have no fear of the past, but beware of what you do in the future. *Neither will I condemn you:* I have blotted out what you have done; now observe what I have commanded, in order to obtain what I have promised."

(Homilies on the Gospel of John 33, 4-6. 8: CCL 36, 307-310)

Augustine (354-430) was born at Thagaste in Africa and received a Christian education, although he was not baptized until 387. In 391 he was ordained priest and in 395 he became coadjutor bishop to Valerius of Hippo, whom he succeeded in 396. Augustine's theology was formulated in the course of his struggle with three heresies: Manicheism, Donatism, and Pelagianism. His writings are voluminous and his influence on subsequent theology immense. He molded the thought of the Middle Ages down to the thirteenth century. Yet he was above all a pastor and a great spiritual writer.

Passion Sunday

Gospel: Luke 19:28-40

Blessed is he who comes in the name of the Lord.

Commentary: Cyril of Alexandria

Behold, a righteous king will reign, and princes will rule with *justice.* The only-begotten Word of God, together with God the Father, has always been king of the universe, and to him all creatures, visible and invisible, are subject. People on earth, having been caught in the snares of sin, were persuaded by the devil to reject his sovereignty and to despise his royal power, but the judge and dispenser of all justice brought them back under his own dominion.

All his ways are straight, says scripture, and by the ways of Christ we mean the divine precepts laid down in the gospel. By observing them we make progress in every virtue, do honor to ourselves by the moral beauty of our lives, and attain the heavenly reward to which we have been called. These are straight, not winding ways: they are direct and easily followed. As it is written, *The way of the upright is straight; the road of the just is made smooth.* Its many decrees make the law a rugged way and its difficulty intolerable, but the way of gospel commands is smooth, without any roughness or steep ascents.

The ways of Christ are straight, then, and as for the holy city, which is the Church, he himself was its builder and he makes it his own dwelling. In other words, he makes the saints his dwelling: sharing as we do in the Holy Spirit, we have Christ within us and have become temples of the living God. Christ is both the founder of the Church and its foundation, and upon this foundation we, like precious stones, are built into a holy temple to become, through the Spirit, a dwelling place for God.

Since it has in Christ such a firm foundation, the Church can never be shaken. Scripture says: *I am laying the foundation stone of Zion, the cornerstone, chosen and precious. No one who believes in him will ever be put to shame.* When he founded the Church, Christ delivered his people from bondage. He saved us from the power of Satan and of sin, freed us and subjected us to his own rule, but not by paying a ransom or by bribes. As one of his disciples wrote, *We have been freed from the futile ways handed down to us by our ancestors, not by anything perishable like silver and gold, but by the precious blood of Christ, like that of a lamb without mark or blemish.* He gave his own blood for us, so that we no longer belong to ourselves, but to him who bought us and saved us. Those therefore who turn aside from the noble rule of the true faith are justly accused by all the saints of denying the Lord who redeemed them.

(On Isaiah IV, 2: PG 70, 967-970)

Cyril of Alexandria (d.444) succeeded his uncle Theophilus as patriarch in 412. Until 428 the pen of this brilliant theologian was employed in exegesis and polemics against the Arians; after that date it was devoted almost entirely to refuting the Nestorian heresy. The teaching of Nestorius was condemned in 431 by the Council of Ephesus at which Cyril presided, and Mary's title, Mother of God, was solemnly recognized. The incarnation is central to Cyril's theology. Only if Christ is consubstantial with the Father and with us can he save us, for the meeting ground between God and ourselves is the flesh of Christ. Through our kinship with Christ, the Word made flesh, we become children of God, and share in the filial relation of the Son with the Father.

Easter Triduum

Evening Mass of the Lord's Supper

Gospel: John 13:1-15

Jesus showed how perfect was his love.

Commentary: Attributed to Augustine of Hippo

This evening we devoutly recall the sacred day before our Lord's passion when he graciously took supper with his disciples, willingly accepting everything that had been written or prophesied concerning his sufferings and death, in his merciful desire to set us free. It behooves us therefore to celebrate such mysteries in a manner befitting their magnitude, so that those of us who desire to share in Christ's sufferings may also deserve to share in his resurrection. For all the mysteries of the Old Testament were fully consummated when Christ handed over to his disciples the bread that was his body and the wine that was his blood, to be offered by them in the eternal mysteries and to be received by each of the faithful for the forgiveness of all sin.

In this way Christ showed that as he suffered for our sake in his mortal body in order to ransom us from eternal death and prepare our way to the heavenly kingdom, so, in order to have us as his companions in eternal life, he would be willing to undergo the same things daily for us whenever we celebrated the sacramental reenactment of these sacred mysteries. For this reason he told his disciples: *Take this, all of you; this is my body, and this the chalice of my blood, which is shed for all for the forgiveness of every sin. Whenever you receive it, you do so in memory of me.*

On the altar, therefore, Christ is present; there he is slain, there he is sacrificed, there his body and blood are received. Christ who on this day gave his disciples the bread and the cup is the same Christ who today consecrates these elements. It is not the man who handles the sacramental species who consecrates Christ's body and blood; it is Christ himself, who was crucified for you. By the lips of the priest the words are pronounced; the body and blood are consecrated by the power and grace of God.

And so in all things let the purity of our mind and thought be evident, for we have a pure and holy sacrifice and must train our souls in a corresponding holiness. Having done all that needs to be done, we may then celebrate these sacred mysteries with all simplicity. Let us therefore approach Christ's altar in a fitting manner, so that we may be counted worthy to share eternal life with Christ, who with the Father and the Holy Spirit lives and reigns for ever and ever. Amen.

(Sermo Mai 143: PLS 2, 1238-1239)

Good Friday

Gospel: John 18:1-19.42

The account of the passion of our Lord Jesus Christ.

Commentary: Peter Chrysologus

The good shepherd lays down his life for his sheep. But what do the sheep gain from the death of their shepherd? We can see from Christ's own death that it leaves the beloved flock a prey to wild beasts, exposed to depredation and slaughter, as indeed the apostles experienced after Jesus had laid down his life for his sheep, consenting to his own murder, and they found themselves uprooted and scattered abroad. The same story is told by the blood of martyrs shed throughout the world, the bodies of Christians thrown to wild beasts, burnt at the stake or flung into rivers: all this suffering was brought about by the death of their shepherd, and his life could have prevented it.

But it is by dying that your shepherd proves his love for you. When danger threatens his sheep and he sees himself unable to protect them, he chooses to die rather than to see calamity overtake his flock. What am I saying? Could Life himself die unless he chose to? Could anyone take life from its author against his will? He himself declared: *I have power to lay down my life, and I have power to take it up again; no one takes it from me.* To die, therefore, was his own choice; immortal though he was, he allowed himself to be put to death.

By allowing himself to be taken captive, he overpowered his opponent; by submitting he overcame him; by his own execution he penalized his enemy, and by dying he opened the door to the conquest of death for his whole flock. And so the Good Shepherd lost none of his sheep when he laid down his life for them; he did not desert them, but kept them safe; he did not abandon them but called them to follow him, leading them by the way of death through the lowlands of this passing world to the pastures of life.

Listen to the shepherd's words: *My sheep hear my voice and follow me.* Those who have followed him to death will inevitably also follow him to life; his companions in shame will be his companions in honor, just as those who have shared his suffering will share his glory. *Where I am,* he says, *there shall my servant be also.* And where is that? Surely in heaven, where Christ is seated at the right hand of God. Do not be troubled, then, because you must live by faith, nor grow weary because hope is deferred. Your reward is certain; it is preserved for you in him who created all things. *You are dead,* scripture says, *and your life is hidden with Christ in God. When Christ your life appears, you too will appear with him in glory.* What was concealed from the farmer at seedtime he will see as he gathers in the sheaves, and the man who plows in sorrow will harvest his crop in gladness.

(Sermon 40: PL 52, 313-314)

Peter Chrysologus (c.400-450), who was born at Imola in Italy, became bishop of Ravenna. He was highly esteemed by the Empress Galla Placidia, in whose presence he preached his first sermon as bishop. He was above all a pastor, and many of his sermons have been preserved.

Easter Vigil

Gospel: Luke 24:1-12

Why look among the dead for someone who is alive?

Commentary: Attributed to Hippolytus of Rome

Now the holy rays of the light of Christ shine forth, the pure stars of the pure Spirit rise, the heavenly treasures of glory and divinity lie open. In this splendor the long dark night has been swallowed up and the dreary shadows of death have vanished. Life is offered to everyone; the whole world is filled with glory. A heavenly light more brilliant than all others sheds its radiance everywhere, and he who was begotten before the morning star and all the stars of heaven, Christ, mighty and immortal, shines upon all creatures more brightly than the sun.

For us who believe in him a glorious day has dawned, a long unending day, the mystical passover symbolically celebrated by the law and effectually accomplished by Christ, a wonderful passover, a miracle of divine virtue, a work of divine power. This is the true festival and the everlasting memorial, the day upon which freedom from suffering comes from suffering, immortality from death, life from the tomb, healing from a wound, resurrection from the fall, and ascension into heaven from the descent into hell. So does God perform his mighty works, bringing the incredible from the impossible to show that he alone can do whatever he wishes.

To show that he had power over death Christ had exercised his royal authority to loose death's bonds even during his lifetime, as for example when he gave the commands, *Lazarus, come out* and *Arise, my child.* For the same reason he surrendered himself completely to death, so that in him that gluttonous beast with his insatiable appetite would die completely. Since *death's power comes from sin,* it searched everywhere in his sinless body for its accustomed food, for sensuality, pride, disobedience or, in a word, for that ancient sin which was its original sustenance. In him, however, it found nothing to feed on and so, being entirely closed in upon itself and destroyed for lack of nourishment, death became its own death.

Many of the just, proclaiming the Good News and prophesying were awaiting him who was to become by his resurrection *the firstborn from the dead.* And so, to save all members of the human race, whether they lived before the law, under the law, or after his own coming, Christ dwelt three days beneath the earth.

After his resurrection it was the women who were the first to see him, for as a woman brought the first sin into the world, so a woman first announced the news of life to the world. Thus they heard the holy words, *Women, rejoice,* for sadness was to be swallowed up by the joy of the resurrection.

O heavenly bounty, spiritual feast, divine Passover, coming down from heaven to earth and ascending again into heaven! You are the light of the new candles, the brightness of the virgins' lamps. Thanks to you the lamps of souls filled with the oil of Christ are no longer extinguished, for the spiritual and divine fire of love burns in all, in both soul and body.

O God, spiritual and eternal Lord, and Christ, Lord and king, we entreat you to extend your strong protecting hands over your holy Church and over your holy people, for ever devoted to you. Raise high in our defense the trophies of your triumph and grant that we like Moses may sing a hymn of victory, for yours is the glory and the power throughout all ages. Amen.

(Easter Homily: SC 27, 116-118. 164-190)

Easter Sunday

Gospel: John 20:1-9

The teaching of scripture is that he must rise from the dead.

Commentary: Guerric of Igny

Blessed and holy are those who share in the first resurrection. Christ is the firstfruits of those who have fallen asleep and the firstborn from the dead. His resurrection, which is the prototype of all others, has guaranteed the rising of our souls in the first resurrection and of our bodies in the second, for he offers his own risen body to our souls as sacrament and to our bodies as exemplar. Even for our souls Christ's single resurrection has prepared a twofold grace: through the living out of the paschal mystery in our daily lives we rise from the death of sin, and by our joyful celebration of the paschal feast today especially we rouse ourselves from the torpor of sleep. Slothful and halfhearted indeed must that person be who does not feel a thrill of joy, a sense of new life and vigor, at the glad cry: *The Lord is risen!* For myself, when I looked upon the dead Jesus I was overwhelmed by despairing grief, but *in the living God,* as scripture says, *my heart and my flesh rejoice.* It is with no mean profit to faith, no slight dividend of joy, that Jesus returns to me from the tomb, for I recognize the living God where only a little while ago I mourned a dead man. My heart was sorrowing for him as slain, but now that he is risen, not only my heart but my flesh also rejoices in the confident hope of my own resurrection and immortality.

I slept and I arose, Christ says. *Awake* then, my sleeping soul, *and rise from the dead, and Christ will give you light!* As the new sun rises from below, the grace of the resurrection already casts its radiance over the whole world, a radiance reflected in the eyes of those who have watched for him since daybreak, a dawn that ushers in the day of eternity. This is the day that knows no evening, the day whose sun will never set again. Only once has that sun gone down, and now once and for all it has ascended above the heavens, leading death captive in its train.

This is the day that the Lord has made; let us rejoice and be glad. And you also, if you watch daily at the threshold of wisdom, fixing your eyes on the doorway and, like the Magdalen, keeping vigil at the entrance to his tomb, you also will find what she found. You will know that what was written of wisdom was written of Christ: *She hastens to make herself known to those who desire her. Anyone who rises early to seek her will have no trouble; he will find her sitting at his gates.* While it was still dark Mary had come to watch at the tomb, and she found Jesus whom she sought standing there in the flesh. But you must know him now according to the spirit, not according to the flesh, and you can be sure of finding his spiritual presence if you seek him with a desire like hers, and if he observes your persevering prayer. Say then to the Lord Jesus, with Mary's love and longing: *My soul yearns for you in the night; my spirit within me earnestly seeks for you.* Make the psalmist's prayer your own as you say: *O God, my God, I watch for you at morning light; my soul thirsts for you.* Then see if you do not also find yourselves singing with them both: *In the morning fill us with your love; we shall exult and rejoice all our days.*

(Sermon on Easter 3, 1-2: PL 185, 148-149)

Guerric of Igny (c.1070/1080-1157), about whose early life little is known, probably received his education at the cathedral school of Tournai, perhaps under the influence of Odo of Cambrai (1807-1092). He seems to have lived a retired life of prayer and study near the cathedral of Tournai. He paid a visit to Clairvaux to consult Saint Bernard, and is mentioned by him as a novice in a letter to Ogerius in 1125/1256. He became abbot of the Cistercian abbey of Igny, in the diocese of Rheims in 1138. A collection of 54 authentic sermons preached on Sundays and feast days has been edited. Guerric's spirituality was influenced by Origen.

Second Sunday of Easter

Gospel: John 20:19-31

After eight days Jesus came in and stood among them.

Commentary: Augustine of Hippo

My dear people, you, like myself, are well aware that our Lord and Savior Jesus Christ is the one physician capable of bringing us eternal healing and salvation. We know, too, that it was in order to accomplish this that he took upon himself the weakness of our human nature, otherwise that weakness would have remained with us for ever. He equipped himself with a human body liable to death, so that in and through that body he might conquer death itself. And though, as the apostle tells us, it was his human weakness that made it possible for him to be crucified, it was his divine power that enabled him to return to life.

The same apostle says: *He will never die again, neither will death have any further hold upon him.* All this you already know and believe, and also the consequences flowing from it; we can be sure that the miracles he wrought while he lived among us were meant to encourage us to accept gifts from him that should never pass away nor have an end. Thus he gave back sight to blind eyes that would shortly be closed again in death; he raised Lazarus from the dead only for him to die again. His bodily cures, indeed, were never meant to last for ever, even though at the end of time he is to give the body itself life everlasting. But because "seeing is believing," he used those visible wonders to build up people's faith in even greater marvels that could not be seen.

Let no one then be found to say that since Christ Jesus our Lord no longer works such miracles among us, the Church was better off in its early days. On the contrary, in one recorded testament, the same Lord sets those who have never seen and yet believe before those who believe only because they see. Indeed, so great was the disciples' weakness at that time, that when they saw the Lord they found it necessary to touch him before they could believe he had really risen from the dead. They were unable to believe the testimony of their own eyes, until they had handled his body and explored his recent wounds with their fingers. Only after this was done could that most hesitant of all his disciples exclaim: *My Lord and my God!* Thus it was by his wounds that Christ, who had so often healed the manifold wounds of others, came to be recognized himself.

Now we may ask: could not the Lord have risen with a body from which all marks of wounds had been erased? No doubt he could have; but he knew his disciples bore within their hearts a wound so deep that the only way to cure it was to retain the scars of his own wounds in his body. And when that confession: *My Lord and my God!* was uttered, what was his answer to it? *You believe,* he said, *because you have seen me; blessed are those who have not seen and yet believe.*

And who, my brothers and sisters, are those if not ourselves and those who are to follow after us? When, later on, the Lord had departed from human sight and faith had had time to strike roots into people's hearts, those who believed in him made their act of faith without seeing him in whom they made it. The faith of such believers is highly meritorious, for it springs from a devoted heart rather than from an exploring hand.

(Sermon 88, 1-2: PL 38, 539-540)

Augustine (354-430) was born at Thagaste in Africa and received a Christian education, although he was not baptized until 387. In 391 he was ordained priest and in 395 he became coadjutor bishop to Valerius of Hippo, whom he succeeded in 396. Augustine's theology was formulated in the course of his struggle with three heresies: Manicheism, Donatism, and Pelagianism. His writings are voluminous and his influence on subsequent theology immense. He molded the thought of the Middle Ages down to the thirteenth century. Yet he was above all a pastor and a great spiritual writer.

Third Sunday of Easter

Gospel: John 21:1-19 or 1-14

Jesus stepped forward, took the bread and gave it to them, and did the same with the fish.

Commentary: Augustine of Hippo

The Lord appeared once again to his disciples after his resurrection, and questioning Peter, who from fear had thrice denied him, extracted from him a threefold declaration of love. Christ had been raised to life in the flesh, and Peter to life in the spirit; for when Christ died as a result of the torments he endured, Peter was also dead as a result of denying his master. Christ the Lord was raised from the dead; Christ the Lord raised up Peter through Peter's love for him. And having obtained from him the assurance of that love, he entrusted his sheep to Peter's care.

We may wonder what advantage there could be for Christ in Peter's love for him. If Christ loves you, you profit, not Christ; and if you love him, again the advantage is yours, not his. But wishing to show us how we should demonstrate our love for him, Christ the Lord made it plain that it is by our concern for his sheep. *Do you love me?,* he asked. *I do love you. Then feed my sheep.* Once, twice, and a third time the same dialogue was repeated. To the Lord's one and only question, Peter had no other answer than *I do love you.* And each time the Lord gave Peter the same command: *Feed my sheep.* Let us love one another then, and by so doing we shall be loving Christ.

Christ, the eternal God, was born in time as man. A true member of the human race, he appeared as one of us; but as God in human form he performed many wonderful signs. As a human being, he suffered much from other human beings; but as God in human form he rose from the dead. For forty days he lived on earth as one of us; then, before the eyes of his disciples, he ascended to heaven, where, as God in human form, he is now seated at the right hand of the Father. We believe all these things, though we have never seen them; we are commanded to love Christ the Lord, whom we have never seen. And we all cry out and say that we love Christ.

But listen to John's words: *If you do not love the brother that you can see, how can you love the God you cannot see?* It is by loving the sheep that you show your love for the shepherd, for the sheep are the members of the shepherd. Indeed, it was to make the sheep members of his own body that the Lord became one of them himself, that he allowed himself to be led like a lamb to the slaughter, and that he allowed the Baptist to point him out and say to him: *Behold the Lamb of God, who takes away the sins of the world.* Surely a crushing burden for a lamb! But that lamb possessed tremendous strength. Do you wish to know how much strength was in this lamb? Because the lamb was crucified, the lion was overcome. If he could vanquish the devil by his own death, think with what power he is able to rule the world! May nothing, then, ever be dearer to us than Christ the Lord; let us love him with all our hearts.

(Sermon 229N, 1: PLS 2, 579)

Augustine (354-430) was born at Thagaste in Africa and received a Christian education, although he was not baptized until 387. In 391 he was ordained priest and in 395 he became coadjutor bishop to Valerius of Hippo, whom he succeeded in 396. Augustine's theology was formulated in the course of his struggle with three heresies: Manicheism, Donatism, and Pelagianism. His writings are voluminous and his influence on subsequent theology immense. He molded the thought of the Middle Ages down to the thirteenth century. Yet he was above all a pastor and a great spiritual writer.

Fourth Sunday of Easter

Gospel: John 10:27-30

I give my sheep eternal life.

Commentary: Cyril of Alexandria

The mark of Christ's sheep is their willingness to hear and obey, just as the sign of those who are not his is their disobedience. We take the word "hear" to imply obedience to what has been said. People who hear God are known by him. No one is entirely unknown by God, but to be known in this way is to become his kin. Thus, when Christ says, *I know mine,* he means, "I will receive them, and give them permanent mystical kinship with myself."

It might be said that inasmuch as he has become man, he has made all human beings his kin, since all are members of the same race; we are all united to Christ in a mystical relationship because of his incarnation. Yet those who do not preserve the likeness of his holiness are alienated from him. *My sheep follow me,* says Christ. By a certain God-given grace, believers follow in the footsteps of Christ. No longer subject to the shadows of the law, they obey the commands of Christ, and guided by his words rise through grace to his own dignity, for they are called children of God. When Christ ascends into heaven, they also follow him.

Christ promises his followers as a recompense and reward eternal life, exemption from death and corruption, and from the torments the judge inflicts upon transgressors. By giving life Christ shows that by nature he *is* life. He does not receive it from another, but supplies it from his own resources. And by eternal life we understand not only length of days which all, both good and bad, shall possess after the resurrection, but also the passing of those days in peace and joy.

We may also see in the word "life" a reference to the eucharist, by means of which Christ implants in believers his own life through their sharing in his flesh, according to the text: *He who eats my flesh and drinks my blood has eternal life.*

(On John's Gospel 7: PG 74, 20)

Cyril of Alexandria (d.444) succeeded his uncle Theophilus as patriarch in 412. Until 428 the pen of this brilliant theologian was employed in exegesis and polemics against the Arians; after that date it was devoted almost entirely to refuting the Nestorian heresy. The teaching of Nestorius was condemned in 431 by the Council of Ephesus at which Cyril presided, and Mary's title, Mother of God, was solemnly recognized. The incarnation is central to Cyril's theology. Only if Christ is consubstantial with the Father and with us can he save us, for the meeting ground between God and ourselves is the flesh of Christ. Through our kinship with Christ, the Word made flesh, we become children of God, and share in the filial relation of the Son with the Father.

Fifth Sunday of Easter

Gospel: John 13:31-33.34-35

I give you a new commandment: love one another.

Commentary: Cyril of Alexandria

I give you a new commandment, said Jesus: *love one another.* But how, we might ask, could he call this commandment new? Through Moses, he had said to the people of old: *You shall love the Lord your God with all your heart and with all your mind, and your neighbor as yourself.* Notice what follows. He was not content simply to say, *I give you a new commandment: love one another.* He showed the novelty of his command and how far the love he enjoined surpassed the old conception of mutual love by going on immediately to add: *Love one another as I have loved you.*

To understand the full force of these words, we have to consider how Christ loved us. Then it will be easy to see what is new and different in the commandment we are now given. Paul tells us that *although his nature was divine, he did not cling to his equality with God, but stripped himself of all privilege to assume the condition of a slave. He became as we are, and appearing in human form humbled himself by being obedient even to the extent of dying, dying on a cross.* And elsewhere Paul writes: *Though he was rich, he became poor.*

Do you not see what is new in Christ's love for us? The law commanded people to love their brothers and sisters as they love themselves, but our Lord Jesus Christ loved us more than himself. He who was one in nature with God the Father and his equal would not have descended to our lowly estate, nor endured in his flesh such a better death for us, nor submitted to the blows given him by his enemies, to the shame, the derision, and all the other sufferings that could not possibly be enumerated; nor, being rich, would he have become poor, had he not loved us far more than himself. It was indeed something new for love to go as far as that!

Christ commands us to love as he did, putting neither reputation, nor wealth, nor anything whatever before love of our brothers and sisters. If need be we must even be prepared to face death for our neighbor's salvation as did our Savior's blessed disciples and those who followed in their footsteps. To them the salvation of others mattered more than their own lives and they were ready to do anything or to suffer anything to save souls that were perishing. *I die daily,* said Paul. *Who suffers weakness without my suffering too? Who is made to stumble without my heart blazing with indignation?*

The Savior urged us to practice this love that transcends the law as the foundation of true devotion to God. He knew that only in this way could we become pleasing in God's eyes, and that it was by seeking the beauty of the love implanted in us by himself that we should attain to the highest blessings.

(On John's Gospel 9: PG 74, 161-164)

Cyril of Alexandria (d.444) succeeded his uncle Theophilus as patriarch in 412. Until 428 the pen of this brilliant theologian was employed in exegesis and polemics against the Arians; after that date it was devoted almost entirely to refuting the Nestorian heresy. The teaching of Nestorius was condemned in 431 by the Council of Ephesus at which Cyril presided, and Mary's title, Mother of God, was solemnly recognized. The incarnation is central to Cyril's theology. Only if Christ is consubstantial with the Father and with us can he save us, for the meeting ground between God and ourselves is the flesh of Christ. Through our kinship with Christ, the Word made flesh, we become children of God, and share in the filial relation of the Son with the Father.

Sixth Sunday of Easter

Gospel: John 14:23-29

The Holy Spirit will teach you everything and remind you of all I have said to you.

Commentary: Bernard of Clairvaux

My *Father and I will come to him*—that is to say, to the holy of heart—says the Son of God, *and we will make our home with him.* It seems to me that when the psalmist said to God: *You make your dwelling in the holy place, you who are Israel's praise,* he had no other heaven in mind than the hearts of the saints. The apostle expresses it quite clearly: *Christ lives in our hearts through faith,* he tells us.

Surely it is no wonder that the Lord Jesus gladly makes his home in such a heaven because, unlike the other heavens, he did not bring it into existence by a mere word of command. He descended into the arena to win it; he laid down his life to redeem it. And so after the battle was won he solemnly declared: *This is my resting place for ever and ever; here I have chosen to dwell.* Blessed indeed is the soul to whom the Lord says: *Come, my chosen one, I will set up my throne in you.*

Why, then, are you sorrowful, my soul, and why are you troubled within me? Are you trying to find a place for the Lord within yourself? Who among us can provide a fitting place for the Lord of glory, a place worthy of his majesty! O that I might be counted worthy to worship at his footstool, that I might at least cling to the feet of some saintly soul whom the Lord has chosen to be his dwelling place! However, the Lord has only to anoint my soul with the oil of his mercy for me in my turn to be able to say: *I have run the way of your commandments because you have enlarged my heart.* Then perhaps, even if I cannot usher him into a large and richly furnished room in my heart where he may refresh himself with his disciples, I shall at least be able to offer him a place to lay his head.

It is necessary for a soul to grow and be enlarged until it is capable of containing God within itself. But the dimensions of a soul are in proportion to its love, as the apostle confirms when he urges the Corinthians to *widen their hearts in love.* Although the soul, being spiritual, cannot be measured physically, grace confers on it what nature does not bestow. It expands spiritually as it makes progress toward human perfection, which is measured by nothing less than the full stature of Christ, and so it grows into a temple sacred to the Lord.

Love, then, is the measure of the soul. Souls are large that love much, small that love little; while as for the soul that has no love at all, such a soul is itself nothing. *Without love,* says Saint Paul, *I am nothing.*

(On the Song of Songs 27, 8-10: Edit. Cist. 1 [1957] 187-189)

Bernard (1090-1153) entered the monastery of Citeaux with thirty companions in 1112. He received his monastic training under the abbot, Saint Stephen Harding, who sent him in 1115 to make a foundation at Clairvaux in France. Soon one of the most influential religious forces in Europe, Bernard was instrumental in founding the Knights Templar and in the election of Pope Innocent I in 1130. He was a strenuous opponent of writers such as Abelard, Gilbert de la Porrée, and Henry of Lausanne. Above all, Bernard was a monk; his sermons and theological writings show an intimate knowledge of scripture, a fine eloquence, and an extraordinarily sublime mysticism.

Ascension

Gospel: Luke 24:46-53

As Jesus blessed them he was carried up to heaven.

Commentary: Cyril of Alexandria

If there had not been many dwelling places in the house of God the Father, our Lord would have told us that he was going on ahead to prepare the dwelling places of the saints. He knew, however, that many such dwelling places already prepared were awaiting the arrival of those who love God. Therefore he did not give this as the reason for his departure, but rather his desire to open the way for our ascent to those heavenly places and to prepare a safe passage for us by making smooth the road that had previously been impassible. For heaven was then completely inaccessible to us—human foot had never trodden that pure and holy country of the angels. It was Christ who first prepared the way for our ascent there. By offering himself to God the Father as the firstfruits of all who are dead and buried, he gave us a way of entry into heaven and was himself the first human being the inhabitants of heaven ever saw. The angels in heaven, knowing nothing of the sacred and profound mystery of the incarnation, were astonished at his coming and almost thrown into confusion by an event so strange and unheard of. *Who is this coming from Edom?* they asked; that is, from the earth. But the Spirit did not leave the heavenly throng ignorant of the wonderful wisdom of God the Father. Commanding them to open the gates of heaven in honor of the King and Master of the universe, he cried out: *Lift up your gates, you princes, and be lifted up you everlasting doors, that the king of glory may come in.*

And so our Lord Jesus Christ has opened up for us a *new and living way,* as Paul says, *not by entering a sanctuary made with hands, but by entering heaven itself to appear before God on our behalf.* For Christ has not ascended in order to make his own appearance before

God the Father. He was, is, and ever will be in the Father and in the sight of him from whom he receives his being, for he is his Father's unfailing joy. But now the Word, who had never before been clothed in human nature, has ascended as a man to show himself in a strange and unfamiliar fashion. And he has done this on our account and in our name, so that being like us, though with his power as the Son, and hearing the command, *Sit at my right hand,* as a member of our race, he might transmit to all of us the glory of being children of God. For since he became man it is as one of us that he sits at the right hand of God the Father, even though he is above all creation and one in substance with his Father, having truly come forth from him as God from God and Light from Light.

As man then he appeared before the Father on our behalf, to enable us whom original sin had excluded from his presence once more to see the Father's face. As the Son he took his seat to enable us as sons and daughters through him to be called children of God. So Paul, who claims to speak for Christ, teaching that the whole human race has a share in the events of Christ's life, says that *God has raised us up with him and enthroned us with him in heaven.* To Christ as the Son by nature belongs the prerogative of sitting at the Father's side; this honor can rightly and truly be ascribed to him alone. Yet because his having become man means that he sits there as one who is in all respects like ourselves, as well as being as we believe God from God, in some mysterious way he passes this honor on to us.

(On John's Gospel 9: PG 74, 182-183)

Cyril of Alexandria (d.444) succeeded his uncle Theophilus as patriarch in 412. Until 428 the pen of this brilliant theologian was employed in exegesis and polemics against the Arians; after that date it was devoted almost entirely to refuting the Nestorian heresy. The teaching of Nestorius was condemned in 431 by the Council of Ephesus at which Cyril presided, and Mary's title, Mother of God, was solemnly recognized. The incarnation is central to Cyril's theology. Only if Christ is consubstantial with the Father and with us can he save us, for the meeting ground between God and ourselves is the flesh of Christ. Through our kinship with Christ, the Word made flesh, we become children of God, and share in the filial relation of the Son with the Father.

Seventh Sunday of Easter

Gospel: John 17:20-26

Father, may them be one in us!

Commentary: Cyril of Alexandria

Our Lord Jesus Christ did not pray only for the twelve disciples. He prayed for all in every age whom their exhortation would persuade to become holy by believing and to be purified by sharing in the Holy Spirit. *May they all be one,* he prayed. *As you Father are in me and I am in you, may they also be one in us.*

The only Son shines out from the very substance of the Father and possesses the Father completely in his own nature. He became man, according to the scriptures, blending himself, so to speak, with our nature by an inexplicable union with an earthly body. In himself he somehow united totally disparate natures to make us sharers in the divine nature.

The communion and abiding presence of the Spirit has passed even to ourselves. This was experienced first through Christ and in Christ when he was seen to have become like us, that is, a human being anointed and sanctified. By nature however he was God, for he proceeded from the Father. It was with his own Spirit that he sanctified the temple of his body and also, in a way befitting it, the world of his creation. Through the mystery of Christ, then, sharing in the Holy Spirit and union with God has become possible also for us, for we are all sanctified in him.

By his own wisdom and the Father's counsel he devised a way of bringing us all together and blending us into a unity with God and one another, even though the differences between us give us each in both body and soul a separate identity. For in holy communion he blesses with one body, which is his own, those who believe in him, and makes them one body with himself and one another. Who could separate those who are united to Christ through that one sacred body, or destroy their true union with one another? If *we all share one loaf* we all become one body, for Christ cannot be divided.

So it is that the Church is the body of Christ and we are its members. For since we are all united to Christ through his sacred body, having received that one indivisible body into our own, our members are not our own but his.

(On John's Gospel 11, 11: PG 74, 553-560)

Cyril of Alexandria (d.444) succeeded his uncle Theophilus as patriarch in 412. Until 428 the pen of this brilliant theologian was employed in exegesis and polemics against the Arians; after that date it was devoted almost entirely to refuting the Nestorian heresy. The teaching of Nestorius was condemned in 431 by the Council of Ephesus at which Cyril presided, and Mary's title, Mother of God, was solemnly recognized. The incarnation is central to Cyril's theology. Only if Christ is consubstantial with the Father and with us can he save us, for the meeting ground between God and ourselves is the flesh of Christ. Through our kinship with Christ, the Word made flesh, we become children of God, and share in the filial relation of the Son with the Father.

Pentecost Sunday

Gospel: John 20:19-23

As the Father sent me, so I am sending you: receive the Holy Spirit.

Commentary: Leo the Great

Every Catholic knows that today's solemnity ranks as one of the principal feasts of the Church. The reverence due to it is beyond all question, because this day is consecrated by the most sublime and wonderful gift of the Holy Spirit. Ten days after the Lord ascended high above the heavens to sit at the right hand of God the Father, and fifty days after his resurrection, on the very same day of the week as this joyful season began, the day of Pentecost has dawned upon us. In itself the feast of Pentecost contains great mysteries relating to the old dispensation as well as to the new, signs which clearly show that grace was heralded by the law and the law fulfilled by grace. Fifty days after the sacrifice of the lamb marking the deliverance of the Hebrews from the Egyptians, the law was given on Mount Sinai; and fifty days from the raising up of Christ after his passion and immolation as the true lamb of God, the Holy Spirit came down upon the apostles and assembled believers. Thus the thoughtful Christian may easily perceive that the origin of the Old Testament laid the foundations of the gospel, and that the Spirit who was the author of the second covenant was the same Spirit who had established the first.

For as the apostles' story testifies, *when the days of Pentecost were fulfilled and all the disciples were together in one place, suddenly there came from heaven a sound like that of a strong driving wind which filled the whole house where they were sitting. And there appeared to them tongues like flames of fire which came to rest on each one of them. And they were all filled with the Holy Spirit and began to speak in other tongues as the Spirit gave them the power of utterance.* O how swift is the word of wisdom, and where God is master how quickly the lesson is learnt! One needs no interpretation in order to understand, no practice in order to gain facility, no time in order to study. *The Spirit* of truth *breathes where he will,* and each nation's own language has become common property in the mouth of the Church.

And so, ever since that day, the clarion call of the gospel has rung out; since the day of Pentecost a rain of charisms, a river of blessings, has watered every desert and dry land, for *the Spirit of God has swept over the waters to renew the face of the earth,* and a blaze of new light has shone out to dispel our former darkness. In the light of those flaming tongues the word of the Lord has shone out clearly, and a fiery eloquence has been enkindled which is charged with the energy to enlighten, the ability to create understanding, and the power to burn away sin and destroy it.

(Sermon 75, 1-3: CCL 138A, 465-468)

Leo the Great (c.400-461) was elected pope in 440. At a time of general disorder he did much to strengthen the influence of the Roman see. Although he was not a profound theologian, Leo's teaching is clear and forceful. His Tome was accepted as a statement of Christological orthodoxy at the Council of Chalcedon (451). One hundred and forty-three of his letters and ninety-six sermons have survived. The latter cover the whole of the liturgical year.

Trinity Sunday

Gospel: John 16:12-15

Whatever the Father has is mine.

Commentary: Hilary of Poitiers

A ccording to the apostle, Lord, your Holy Spirit fully understands and penetrates your inmost depths; he also intercedes on my behalf, saying to you things for which I cannot find the words. Nothing can penetrate your being but what is divine already; nor can the depths of your immense majesty be measured by any power which itself is alien or extrinsic to you. So, whatever enters into you is yours already, nor can anything which has the power to search your very depths ever have been other than your own.

Your Holy Spirit proceeds through your Son from you; though I may fail to grasp the full meaning of that statement, I give it nonetheless the firm assent of my mind and heart.

I may indeed show dullness and stupidity in my understanding of these spiritual matters; it is as your only Son has said: *Do not be surprised if I have said to you: You must be born again. Just as the wind blows where it pleases and you hear the sound of it without knowing where it is coming from or going to, so will it be with everyone who is born again of water and the Holy Spirit.* By my regeneration I have received the faith, but I am still ignorant; and yet I have a firm hold on something which I do not understand. I am born again, capable of rebirth but without conscious perception of it. The Spirit abides by no rules; he speaks when he pleases, what he pleases, and where he pleases. We are conscious of his presence when he comes, but the reasons for his approach or his departure remain hidden from us.

John tells us that all things came into being through the Son who is God the Word abiding with you, Father, from the beginning. Paul in his turn enumerates the things created in the Son, both visible and invisible, in heaven and on earth. And while he is specific about all that was created in and through Christ, of the Holy Spirit he considers it enough simply to say that he is your Spirit.

Therefore I concur with those chosen men in thinking that just as it is not expedient for me to venture beyond my mental limitation and predicate anything of your only begotten Son save that, as those witnesses have assured us, he was born of you, so it is not fitting for me to go beyond the power of human thought and the teaching of those same witnesses by declaring anything regarding the Holy Spirit other than that he is your Spirit. Rather than waste time in a fruitless war of words, I would prefer to spend it in the firm profession of an unhesitating faith.

I beg you therefore, Father, to preserve in me that pure and reverent faith and to grant that to my last breath I may testify to my conviction. May I always hold fast to what I publicly professed in the creed when I was baptized in the name of the Father and of the Son and of the Holy Spirit. May I worship you, the Father of us all, and your Son together with you and may I be counted worthy to receive your Holy Spirit who through your only Son proceeds from you. For me there is sufficient evidence for this faith in the words: *Father, all that I have is yours, and all that is yours is mine,* spoken by Jesus Christ my Lord who remains, in and from and with you, the God who is blessed for endless ages. Amen.

(The Trinity XII, 55-56: PL 10, 468-472)

Hilary (315-367) was elected bishop of Poitiers in 353. Because of his struggles with the Arians and his treatise on the Trinity, for which he was exiled, he has been called "the Athanasius of the West." He also wrote a commentary on Saint Matthew's gospel and another on a selection of the psalms. His style is difficult and obscure and he makes much use of allegory.

Corpus Christi

Gospel: Luke 9:11-17

They all ate and were filled.

Commentary: John Chrysostom

Christ gave us his flesh to eat in order to deepen our love for him. When we approach him, then, there should be burning within us a fire of love and longing. Otherwise the punishment awaiting us will be in proportion to the magnitude of the graces we have received and of which we have shown ourselves unworthy.

The wise men paid homage to Christ's body even when it was lying in a manger. Foreigners who did not worship the true God left their homes and their native land, set out on a long journey, and on reaching its end, worshiped in great fear and trembling. Let us, the citizens of heaven, at least imitate these foreigners. They only saw Christ in a manger, they saw nothing of what you now see, and yet they approached him with profound awe and reverence. You see him, not in a manger but on an altar, not carried by a woman but offered by a priest; and you see the Spirit bountifully poured out upon the offerings of bread and wine. Unlike the wise men, you do not merely see Christ's body: you know his power as well, and whole divine plan for our salvation. Having been carefully instructed, you are ignorant of none of the marvels he has performed. Let us then awaken in ourselves a feeling of awe and let us show a far greater reverence than did those foreigners, for we shall bring down fire upon our heads if we approach this sacrament casually, without thinking of what we do.

By saying this I do not mean that we should not approach it, but simply that we should not do so thoughtlessly. Just as coming to it in a casual way is perilous, so failing to share in this sacramental meal is hunger and death. This food strengthens us; it emboldens us to speak freely to our God; it is our hope, our salvation, our light, and our life.

If we go to the next world fortified by this sacrifice, we shall enter its sacred portals with perfect confidence, as though protected all over by armor of gold.

But why do I speak of the next world? Because of this sacrament earth becomes heaven for you. Throw open the gates of heaven—or rather, not of heaven but of the heaven of heavens—look through and you will see the proof of what I say. What is heaven's most precious possession? I will show you it here on earth. I do not show you angels or archangels, heaven or the heaven of heavens, but I show you the very Lord of all these. Do you not see how you gaze, here on earth, upon what is most precious of all? You not only gaze on it, but touch it as well. You not only touch it, but even eat it, and take it away with you to your homes. It is essential therefore when you wish to receive this sacrament to cleanse your soul from sin and to prepare your mind.

*(Homilies on the First Letter to the Corinthians
24, 4: PG 61, 204-205)*

John Chrysostom (c.347-407) was born at Antioch and studied under Diodore of Tarsus, the leader of the Antiochene school of theology. After a period of great austerity as a hermit, he returned to Antioch where he was ordained deacon in 381 and priest in 386. From 386 to 397 it was his duty to preach in the principal church of the city, and his best homilies, which earned him the title "Chrysostomos" or "the golden-mouthed," were preached at this time. In 397 Chrysostom became patriarch of Constantinople, where his efforts to reform the court, clergy, and people led to his exile in 404 and finally to his death from the hardships imposed on him. Chrysostom stressed the divinity of Christ against the Arians and his full humanity against the Apollinarians, but he had no speculative bent. He was above all a pastor of souls, and was one of the most attractive personalities of the early Church.

Sacred Heart

Gospel: Luke 15:3-7

Share my joy; I have found my lost sheep.

Commentary: Ambrose of Milan

The Lord Jesus himself declared that the shepherd in the gospel left the ninety-sheep and went after the one that had strayed. The lost sheep he spoke of was the hundredth. Now the number one hundred stands for perfection and fullness, and there should be a lesson in this for you. There are grounds for preferring the stray sheep to the others. The truth is that it is a greater thing to turn back from one's sins than scarcely to have committed any. When souls are steeped in sin, not only do they need perfect human virtue to shake off the tyranny of lust and mend their ways, but heavenly grace is also necessary. A person can make a resolution to amend in the future, but forgiveness of the past is a matter for divine power.

When the shepherd has at last found the sheep, he places it on his shoulders. I am sure you are aware of the symbolism contained in the way the weary sheep is revived; how it represents humanity, worn out and exhausted, incapable of restoration to health except by the mystery of the passion and blood of our Lord Jesus Christ, of whom it is written that the *symbol of dominion will be upon his shoulders.* For it was on the cross that he bore our infirmities, canceling upon it the sins of the whole world. The angels have good reason to rejoice, seeing the lost sheep straying no longer, seeing him, in fact, giving no further thought to wandering.

Like a lost sheep I have gone astray; give life to your servant, for I do not forget your commandments. I am your servant, Lord; come in search of me, for unless the shepherd seeks out the stray, it will die. Return is still possible for the one who is lost; he can still be recalled to the right path. Come, then, Lord Jesus, seek your servant, seek your exhausted sheep. Come as shepherd of the flock, seeking your sheep as Joseph sought his, the sheep that went astray while you were lingering in the mountains. Leave your ninety-nine sheep there and come in search of the one that is lost. Come, not with rod in hand, but in a spirit of love and gentleness.

Seek me, Lord; I need you. Seek me, find me, lift me up, carry me. You are expert at finding what you search for; and when you have found the stray you stoop down, lift him up, and place him on your own shoulders. To you he is a burden of love, not an object of revulsion; it is no irksome task to you to bring justification to the human race. Come then, Lord; I have gone astray, but *I have not forgotten your commandments.* I still hold on to the hope of healing. Come, Lord; none but you can bring back your erring sheep. Those whom you leave behind will not be grieved, because the sinner's return will be a joy to them too. Come, do your saving work on earth, and let there be joy in heaven.

Come in search of your sheep, not through the ministry of servants or hirelings, but in your own person. Take my human nature, which fell in Adam. Take my humanity, not from Sarah but from the spotless Virgin Mary, a virgin preserved through your grace from any stain of sin. Bear me on the cross where sinners find salvation, where alone there is rest for the weary, where alone there is life for the dying.

(Commentary on Psalm 119 (118) 22, III, 27-30:
CSEL 62, 489.502-504)

Ambrose (339-397) was born in Trier, the son of a praetorian prefect of Gaul. On the death of Auxentius, the Arian bishop of Milan, Ambrose, while still a catechumen, was elected to the see by acclamation. We know from Saint Augustine that as bishop he was accessible to everyone. Although Ambrose was influenced by the Greek Fathers, especially Origen, his preaching had the practical bent characteristic of Western theological writers.

Second Sunday in Ordinary Time

Gospel: John 2:1-12

The first of the signs given by Jesus was at Cana in Galilee.

Commentary: Attributed to Maximus of Turin

The Son of God went to the wedding so that marriage, which had been instituted by his own authority, might be sanctified by his blessed presence. He went to a wedding of the old order when he was about to take a new bride for himself through the conversion of the Gentiles, a bride who would for ever remain a virgin. He went to a wedding even though he himself was not born of human wedlock. He went to the wedding not, certainly, to enjoy a banquet, but rather to make himself known by miracles. He went to the wedding not to drink wine, but to give it, for when there was none left for the wedding guests, the most blessed Mary said to him: *They have no wine.*

Jesus answered as though he were displeased. *Woman,* he said, *is that my concern, or yours?* It can hardly be doubted that these were words of displeasure. However, this I think was only because his mother mentioned to him so casually the lack of earthly wine, when he had come to offer the peoples of the whole world the new chalice of eternal salvation. By his reply, *My hour has not yet come,* he was foretelling the most glorious hour of his passion, and the wine of our redemption which would obtain life for all. Mary was asking for a temporal favor, but Christ was preparing joys that would be eternal. Nevertheless, the Lord in his goodness did not refuse this small grace while great graces were awaited.

Holy Mary, therefore, since she was in very truth the Mother of the Lord, and in her spirit knew in advance what would happen and foresaw the Lord's will, took care to advise the servants to do whatever he told them. Of course this holy Mother knew that the rebuke of her

Son and Lord was not an insult born of anger, but that it contained a mysterious compassion.

Then, to save his Mother from embarrassment because of his reproach, the Lord revealed his sovereign power. Addressing the expectant servants he said: *Fill the jars with water.* The servants promptly obeyed, and suddenly in a marvelous way the water began to acquire potency, take on color, emit fragrance, and gain flavor—all at once it changed its nature completely!

Now this transformation of the water from its own substance into another testified to the powerful presence of the Creator. Only he who had made it out of nothing could change water into something whose use was quite different. Dearly beloved, have no doubt that he who changed water into wine is the same as he who from the beginning has thickened it into snow and hardened it into ice. It is he who changed it into blood for the Egyptians and bade it flow from the dry rock for the thirsty Hebrews—the rock which, newly transformed into a spring, was like a mother's breast refreshing with its gentle flow a countless multitude of people.

Scripture says that *this sign at Cana in Galilee was the first that Jesus performed. He manifested his glory, and his disciples believed in him.* It was not what they saw happening that the disciples believed, but what could not be seen by bodily eyes. They did not believe that Jesus Christ was the son of the Virgin—that was something they knew. Rather they believed that he was the only Son of the Most High, as this miracle proved.

And so let us too believe wholeheartedly that he whom we confess to be the Son of Man is also the Son of God. Let us believe not only that he shared our nature, but also that he was consubstantial with the Father; for as a man he was present at the wedding, and as God he changed the water into wine. If such is our faith, the Lord will give us also to drink of the sobering wine of his grace.

(Sermon 23: PL 57, 274-276)

Third Sunday
in Ordinary Time

Gospel: Luke 1:1-4; 4:14-21

Today this text is being fulfilled.

Commentary: Origen of Alexandria

Jesus returned to Galilee in the power of the Spirit, and his reputation spread throughout the countryside. He taught in their synagogues and everyone sang his praises.

When you read about Jesus teaching in the synagogues of Galilee and everyone there praising him, take care not to regard those people as uniquely privileged, and yourselves as deprived of his teaching. If scripture is true, it was not only to the Jewish congregations of his own generation that our Lord spoke. He still speaks to us assembled here today—and not only to us, but to other congregations also. Throughout the world Jesus looks for instruments through which he can continue his teaching. Pray that I may be one of them, and that he may find me ready and fit to sing his praises.

Then Jesus came to Nazareth, where he had been brought up, and went into the synagogue on the sabbath day as was his custom. When he stood up to read they handed him the scroll of the prophet Isaiah. Unrolling the scroll he found the place where it is written, "The Spirit of the Lord has been given to me, for he has anointed me."

It was no coincidence, but in accordance with the plan of divine providence, that Jesus unrolled the scroll and found in it this chapter prophesying about himself. Since it is written: *Not a single sparrow will fall to the ground without your Father's permission,* and the apostles were told that every hair on their heads had been counted, we can be sure it was not by chance that the scroll of the prophet Isaiah was produced rather than some other and this precise passage found which speaks of the mystery of Christ: *The Spirit of the Lord has been given to me, for he has anointed me.*

When Jesus had read this prophecy, *he rolled up the scroll, handed it back to the assistant and sat down. Every eye in the synagogue was fixed upon him.*

Here too in this synagogue, that is in this present assembly, you can at this very moment fix your eyes upon your Savior if you wish. Whenever you direct your inward gaze toward wisdom and truth and the contemplation of God's only Son, then your eyes are fixed upon Jesus. Blessed was that congregation of which the gospel says, *All eyes in the synagogue were fixed upon him!* How I long for our own assembly to deserve the same testimony; for all of you, catechumens as well as the faithful, women, men, and children, to have your eyes, not those of the body but of the soul, turned toward Jesus! When you look at Jesus your own faces will become radiant with his reflected glory, and you will be able to say: *The light of your face has shed its brightness upon us, O Lord!* To you be glory and power for ever and ever! Amen.

(On Luke's Gospel 32, 2-6: SC 87, 386-392)

Origen (183-253), one of the greatest thinkers of ancient times, became head of the catechetical school of Alexandria at the age of eighteen. In 230 he was ordained priest by the bishop of Caesarea. His life was entirely devoted to the study of scripture and he was also a great master of the spiritual life. His book *On First Principles* was the first great theological synthesis. Many of his works are extant only in Latin as a result of his posthumous condemnation for heterodox teaching. Nevertheless, in intention he was always a loyal son of the Church.

Fourth Sunday
in Ordinary Time

Gospel: Luke 4:21-30

Jesus, like Elijah and Elisha, was not sent only to the Jews.

Commentary: Cyril of Alexandria

Desiring to win over the whole world and bring its inhabitants to God the Father, raising all things to a higher condition and, in a sense, renewing the face of the earth, the Lord of the universe took the form of a servant and brought the good news to the poor. This, he said, was why he had been sent.

Now by the poor we may understand those who were then deprived of all spiritual blessings and who lived in the world without hope and without God, as scripture says. They are those among the Gentiles who, enriched by faith in Christ, have gained the divine, the heavenly treasure, which is the saving proclamation of the gospel. Through this they have become sharers in the kingdom of heaven and companions of the saints. They have inherited blessings impossible to express or comprehend, for *eye has not seen,* says scripture, *nor ear heard, nor human heart conceived what God has prepared for those who love him.*

To the brokenhearted Christ promises healing and release, and to the blind he gives sight. For those who worship created things, and say to a piece of wood, *"You are my father,"* and to a stone, *"you gave me birth,"* thus failing to recognize him who is really and truly God, are they not blind? Are not their hearts devoid of the spiritual and divine light? To these the Father sends the light of true knowledge of God. Having been called by faith, they know God, or rather, they are known by him. They were children of night and of darkness, but they have become children of light. The Day has shone upon them, the Sun of Righteousness has risen, the Morning Star has appeared in all its brilliance.

All that has been said, however, could also be applied to the Israelites, for they too were poor, brokenhearted, captives in a certain sense, and in darkness. But Christ came, and it was to the Israelites first that he made known the purpose of his coming: he came to proclaim the acceptable year of the Lord, and the day of retribution. That was the acceptable year, when Christ was crucified for us, for then we became acceptable to God the Father. Through Christ we bear fruit, as he himself taught us when he said: *I tell you truly that unless a grain of wheat falls into the ground and dies, it remains as it is, a single grain; but if it dies, it bears a rich harvest;* and again: *When I am lifted up from the earth, I will draw the whole world to myself.* Moreover, on the third day he came to life again, after trampling death's power underfoot. He then addressed these words to his disciples: *All power has been given to me in heaven and on earth. Go and make disciples of all nations, baptizing them in the name of the Father, and of the Son, and of the Holy Spirit.*

(On Isaiah 5, 5: PG 70, 1352-1353)

Cyril of Alexandria (d.444) succeeded his uncle Theophilus as patriarch in 412. Until 428 the pen of this brilliant theologian was employed in exegesis and polemics against the Arians; after that date it was devoted almost entirely to refuting the Nestorian heresy. The teaching of Nestorius was condemned in 431 by the Council of Ephesus at which Cyril presided, and Mary's title, Mother of God, was solemnly recognized. The incarnation is central to Cyril's theology. Only if Christ is consubstantial with the Father and with us can he save us, for the meeting ground between God and ourselves is the flesh of Christ. Through our kinship with Christ, the Word made flesh, we become children of God, and share in the filial relation of the Son with the Father.

Fifth Sunday
in Ordinary Time

Gospel: Luke 5:1-11

They left everything and followed him.

Commentary: Augustine of Hippo

While he was on the mountain with Christ the Lord in company with the two other disciples James and John, the blessed apostle Peter heard a voice from heaven saying: *This is my beloved Son, in whom I am well pleased. Listen to him.* The apostle remembered this and made it known in his letter. *We heard a voice coming from heaven,* he said, *when we were with him on the holy mountain;* and he added: *so we have confirmation of what was prophesied. A voice came from heaven, and prophecy was confirmed.*

How great was Christ's courtesy! This Peter who spoke these words was once a fisherman, and in our day a public speaker deserves high praise if he is able to converse with a fisherman! Addressing the first Christians the apostle Paul says: *Brothers and sisters, remember what you were when you were called. Not many of you were wise according to human standards; not many of you were influential or of noble birth. But God chose what the world regards as weak in order to disconcert the strong; God chose what the world regards as foolish in order to abash the wise; God chose what the world regards as common and contemptible, of no account whatever, in order to overthrow the existing order.*

If Christ had first chosen a man skilled in public speaking, such a man might well have said: "I have been chosen on account of my eloquence." If he had chosen a senator, the senator might have said: "I have been chosen because of my rank." If his first choice had been an emperor, the emperor surely might have said: "I have been chosen for the sake of the power I have at my disposal." Let these worthies keep quiet and defer to others; let them hold their peace for a while. I am not saying they should be passed over or despised; I am simply asking all those who can find any grounds for pride in what they are to give way to others just a little.

Christ says: Give me this fisherman, this man without education or experience, this man to whom no senator would deign to speak, not even if he were buying fish. Yes, give me him; once I have taken possession of him, it will be obvious that it is I who am at work in him. Although I mean to include senators, orators, and emperors among my recruits, even when I have won over the senator I shall still be surer of the fisherman. The senator can always take pride in what he is; so can the orator and the emperor, but the fisherman can glory in nothing except Christ alone. Any of these other men may come and take lessons from me in the importance of humility for salvation, but let the fisherman come first. He is the best person to win over an emperor.

Remember this fisherman, then, this holy, just, good, Christ-filled fisherman. In his nets cast throughout the world he has the task of catching this nation as well as all the others. So remember that claim of his: *We have confirmation of what was prophesied.*

(Sermon 43, 5-7: CCL 41, 510-511)

Augustine (354-430) was born at Thagaste in Africa and received a Christian education, although he was not baptized until 387. In 391 he was ordained priest and in 395 he became coadjutor bishop to Valerius of Hippo, whom he succeeded in 396. Augustine's theology was formulated in the course of his struggle with three heresies: Manicheism, Donatism, and Pelagianism. His writings are voluminous and his influence on subsequent theology immense. He molded the thought of the Middle Ages down to the thirteenth century. Yet he was above all a pastor and a great spiritual writer.

Sixth Sunday
in Ordinary Time

Gospel: Luke 6:17.20-26

Happy are you who are poor. Alas for you who are rich.

Commentary: John Chrysostom

Only Christians have a true sense of values; their joys and sorrows are not the same as other people's. The sight of a wounded boxer wearing a victor's crown would make someone ignorant of the games think only of the boxer's wounds and how painful they must be. Such a person would know nothing of the happiness the crown gives. And it is the same when people see the things we suffer without knowing why we do so. It naturally seems to them to be suffering pure and simple. They see us struggling and facing danger, but beyond their vision are the rewards, the crowns of victory—all we hope to gain through the contest!

When Paul said, *We possess nothing, and yet we have everything,* what did he mean by "everything"? Wealth of both the earthly and the spiritual order. Did he not possess every earthly gift when whole cities received him as an angel, when people were ready to pluck out their eyes for him, or bare their necks to the sword? But if you would think of spiritual blessings, you will see that it was in these above all that he was rich. The King of the universe and Lord of angels loved him so much that he shared his secrets with him. Did he not surpass all others in wealth then? Did he not possess all things? Had it been otherwise, demons would not have been subject to him, nor sickness and suffering put to flight by his presence.

We too, then, when we suffer anything for Christ's sake, should do so not only with courage, but even with joy. If we have to go hungry, let us be glad as if we were at a banquet. If we are insulted, let us be elated as though we had been showered with praises. If we lose all we possess, let us consider ourselves the gainers. If we provide for the poor, let us regard ourselves as the recipients. Anyone who does not give in this way will find it difficult to give at all. So when you wish to distribute alms, do not think only of what you are giving away; think rather of what you are gaining, for your gain will exceed your loss.

And not only in the matter of almsgiving, but also with every virtue you practice: do not think of the painful effort involved, but of the sweetness of the reward; and above all remember that your struggles are for the sake of our Lord Jesus. Then you will easily rise above them, and live out your whole lifetime in happiness; for nothing brings more happiness than a good conscience.

(Homily on Second Corinthians 12, 4: Bareille, t. 17, 480-481)

John Chrysostom (c.347-407) was born at Antioch and studied under Diodore of Tarsus, the leader of the Antiochene school of theology. After a period of great austerity as a hermit, he returned to Antioch where he was ordained deacon in 381 and priest in 386. From 386 to 397 it was his duty to preach in the principal church of the city, and his best homilies, which earned him the title "Chrysostomos" or "the golden-mouthed," were preached at this time. In 397 Chrysostom became patriarch of Constantinople, where his efforts to reform the court, clergy, and people led to his exile in 404 and finally to his death from the hardships imposed on him. Chrysostom stressed the divinity of Christ against the Arians and his full humanity against the Apollinarians, but he had no speculative bent. He was above all a pastor of souls, and was one of the most attractive personalities of the early Church.

Seventh Sunday
in Ordinary Time

Gospel: Luke 6:27-38

Be merciful as your Father is merciful.

Commentary: Augustine of Hippo

All the ways of the Lord are mercy and faithfulness, for those who keep his covenant and will. We have here a tremendous statement on the subject of faithfulness and mercy. Mercy is mentioned because it is not our deserts but his own goodness that God regards. He forgives us all our sins and promises us eternal life. But it also speaks of faithfulness, because God never fails to honor his promises. Acknowledging this to be so, let us practice these virtues ourselves in our present circumstances. Just as God has shown us his mercy and faithfulness—his mercy by forgiving our sins and his faithfulness by keeping his promises—so we too should practice mercy and faithfulness in our own lives. Let us show mercy to the sick and needy, even our enemies, and practice faithfulness by refraining from sin. Never let us add sin to sin, because whoever presumes too much on God's mercy has secretly consented to the suggestion that he can cause God to be unjust. Such a person imagines that even if he persists in sin and refuses to give up his wrongdoing, God will still come and give him a place among his obedient servants.

Would this be justice, for God to assign an obstinate sinner like you the same place as those who have turned their backs on sin? Would you be so unjust as to expect God to be unjust too? Why then are you trying to bend God to your will? Bend yourself, rather, to his. Yet how many people do, in fact, bend their wills to God's? Only those few of whom it is said: *The one who perseveres to the end will be saved.*

It is with good reason that scripture asks: *Who will seek God's mercy and faithfulness for his own sake?* What precisely does *for his own sake* mean? Surely it would have been enough to say *Who will seek* without adding *for his own sake.*

The answer is that many people seek to discover God's mercy and faithfulness from the sacred books, and yet, when their learning is done, they live for their own sakes and not for God's. They are intent on their own interests, not those of Jesus Christ. They preach mercy and faithfulness without practicing them. Their preaching proves that they know their subject, for they would not preach without knowledge. But it is a different matter in the case of someone who loves God and Christ. When such a person preaches God's mercy and faithfulness, he seeks to make them known for God's sake, not his own. This means that he is not out to gain temporal benefits from his preaching; his desire is to help Christ's members, that is, those who believe in him, by faithfully sharing with them the knowledge he himself possesses, so *that the living may no longer live for themselves, but for him who died for all.*

(Expositions of the Psalms 60, 9: CCL 39, 771)

Augustine (354-430) was born at Thagaste in Africa and received a Christian education, although he was not baptized until 387. In 391 he was ordained priest and in 395 he became coadjutor bishop to Valerius of Hippo, whom he succeeded in 396. Augustine's theology was formulated in the course of his struggle with three heresies: Manicheism, Donatism, and Pelagianism. His writings are voluminous and his influence on subsequent theology immense. He molded the thought of the Middle Ages down to the thirteenth century. Yet he was above all a pastor and a great spiritual writer.

Eighth Sunday
in Ordinary Time

Gospel: Luke 6:39-45

One speaks from what is in one's heart.

Commentary: Cyril of Alexandria

The blessed disciples were to be the spiritual guides and teachers of the whole world. It had therefore to be clearly seen by all that they held fast to the true faith. It was essential for them to be familiar with the gospel way of life, skilled in every good work, and to give teaching that was precise, salutary, and scrupulously faithful to the truth they themselves had long pondered, enlightened by the divine radiance. Otherwise they would be blind leaders of the blind. Those imprisoned in the darkness of ignorance can never lead others in the same sorry state to knowledge of the truth. Should they try, both would fall headlong into the ditch of the passions.

To destroy the ostentatious passion of boastfulness and stop people from trying to win greater honor than their teachers, Christ declared: *The disciple is not above his teacher.* Even if some should advance so far as to equal their teachers in holiness, they ought to remain within the limits set by them, and follow their example. Paul also taught this when he said: *Be imitators of me, as I am of Christ.* So then, if the Master does not judge, why are you judging? He came not to judge the world, but to take pity on it.

What he is saying, then, is this: "If I do not pass judgment, neither must you, my disciple. You may be even more guilty of the faults of which you accuse another. Will you not be ashamed when you come to realize this?" The Lord uses another illustration for the same teaching when he says: *Why do you look for the speck in your brother's eye?*

With compelling arguments he persuades us that we should not want to judge others, but should rather examine our own hearts, and strive to expel the passions seated in them, asking this grace from God. He it is who heals the contrite of heart and frees us from our spiritual disorders. If your own sins are greater and worse than other people's, why do you censure them, and neglect what concerns yourself?

This precept, then, is essential for all who wish to live a holy life, and particularly for those who have undertaken the instruction of others. If they are virtuous and self-restrained, giving an example of the gospel way of life by their own actions, they will rebuke those who do not choose to live as they do in a friendly way, so as not to break their own habit of gentleness.

(On Saint Luke 6: PG 72, 602-603)

Cyril of Alexandria (d.444) succeeded his uncle Theophilus as patriarch in 412. Until 428 the pen of this brilliant theologian was employed in exegesis and polemics against the Arians; after that date it was devoted almost entirely to refuting the Nestorian heresy. The teaching of Nestorius was condemned in 431 by the Council of Ephesus at which Cyril presided, and Mary's title, Mother of God, was solemnly recognized. The incarnation is central to Cyril's theology. Only if Christ is consubstantial with the Father and with us can he save us, for the meeting ground between God and ourselves is the flesh of Christ. Through our kinship with Christ, the Word made flesh, we become children of God, and share in the filial relation of the Son with the Father.

Ninth Sunday
in Ordinary Time

Gospel: Luke 7:1-10

Nowhere in Israel have I found as much faith.

Commentary: Augustine of Hippo

In the gospel we heard our own faith extolled as it was manifested by humility. The Lord Jesus agreed to go to the centurion's house to cure his servant, but he replied: *I am not worthy to have you under my roof; only say the word and my servant will be healed.* In protesting his unworthiness the centurion showed himself worthy to have Christ enter not his house but his heart. Yet he could not have said this with such faith and humility unless he already bore within his heart the one he was too overawed to have within his house. In any case, there would have been no great happiness at the entry of the Lord Jesus within his walls if he were not present in his heart. The Master who taught humility by both word and example dined in the house of a certain proud Pharisee called Simon; but though he was in his house, the Son of Man found nowhere in the Pharisee's heart where he could lay his head. The centurion's house he did not in fact enter, but he took possession of his heart. The centurion said: *I am not worthy to have you under my roof.* The Lord praised the faith shown by his humility, replying: *I tell you, not even in Israel have I found faith like this.* He meant Israel in a physical sense, for the centurion was already an Israelite in spirit.

The Lord had come to the people of Israel, that is to the Jews, to seek out the lost sheep first among that people in whom and from whom he had taken flesh; but not even there, he says, did he find such faith. We can only judge a person's faith from a human viewpoint; but he who sees the heart and whom no one ever deceives testified to the state of this man's heart: on hearing the centurion's humble words he pronounced his assurance of healing.

But what emboldened the centurion to act as he did? *I am under authority myself,* he said, *and have soldiers under me; and I say to one man, Go, and he goes; to another, Come here, and he comes; to my servant, Do this, and he does it.* I exercise authority over my subordinates, and am myself subject to those with authority over me. If I then, a man subject to authority, have authority to give orders, what must be the extent of your authority which all authorities obey?

Now the man who said this was a Gentile as well as a centurion. He was a professional soldier and, as a centurion, acted according to his rank: subject to authority and exercising authority, obeying as a subordinate and giving orders to those subordinate to him. As for the Lord, though living among the Jewish people, he was already beginning to make it known that his Church would extend throughout the whole world into which he was about to send his apostles. Although the Gentiles would not see him they would believe in him, whereas the Jewish leaders who saw him would put him to death.

The Lord did not enter the centurion's house in person, but, though absent in body, he was present by his divine power, bringing healing of body and soul. And it was the same with the Gentiles. Only among the Jews was he bodily present. Among no other people was he born of a virgin, among no others did he suffer, travel on foot, endure our human lot, or perform divine wonders. No, he did none of these things among other peoples, and yet the prophecy about him was fulfilled: *People unknown to me served me.* How was that possible if they did not know him? *As soon as they heard of me they obeyed me.* Indeed, the whole world has heard and has obeyed.

(Sermon 62, 1. 3-4: PL 38, 414-416)

Augustine (354-430) was born at Thagaste in Africa and received a Christian education, although he was not baptized until 387. In 391 he was ordained priest and in 395 he became coadjutor bishop to Valerius of Hippo, whom he succeeded in 396. Augustine's theology was formulated in the course of his struggle with three heresies: Manicheism, Donatism, and Pelagianism. His writings are voluminous and his influence on subsequent theology immense. He molded the thought of the Middle Ages down to the thirteenth century. Yet he was above all a pastor and a great spiritual writer.

Tenth Sunday
in Ordinary Time

Gospel: Luke 7:11-17

Young man, I say to you, arise.

Commentary: Augustine of Hippo

All believers are moved when they hear the accounts of the miracles
wrought by Jesus, our Lord and Savior, though they are affected
by them in different ways. Some are astounded at his wonderful
physical cures, but have not yet learned to discern the greater miracles
that lie beyond the world of sense. Others marvel that the miracles that
they hear of our Lord working on people's bodies are now being
accomplished more wonderfully in their souls.

No Christian should doubt that even today the dead are being raised
to life. Yet, while everyone has eyes capable of seeing the dead rise
in the way the widow's son rose, as we have just heard in the gospel,
the ability to see the spiritually dead arise is possessed only by those
who have themselves experienced a spiritual resurrection.

It is a greater thing to raise what will live for ever than to raise what
must die again. When the young man in the gospel was raised, his
widowed mother rejoiced; when souls are daily raised from spiritual
death, mother Church rejoices. The young man was dead in body,
these latter are dead in spirit. Those who witnessed the lad's visible
death mourned openly and visibly, but the invisible death of the dead
in spirit was neither seen nor thought about.

The Lord Jesus sought out those he knew to be dead; he alone knew
they were dead, and he alone could make them live again. Unless he
had come to raise the dead the apostle would not have said: *Rise up.*
Sleeper, of course, makes you think of someone slumbering, but when
the apostle goes on to say *rise from the dead,* you realize that he really
means a dead person. The visibly dead are often said to be sleeping;

and indeed for one who has power to wake them they really are only sleeping. A person is dead as far as you are concerned if he does not waken no matter how much you slap or pinch or even wound him. But for Christ the young man he commanded to rise was only sleeping, because he immediately got up. Christ raises the dead from their graves more easily than another can rouse a sleeper from his bed.

Our Lord Jesus Christ wished us to understand that what he did for people's bodies he also did for their souls. He did not work miracles merely for miracles' sake; his object was that his deeds might arouse wonder in the beholders and reveal the truth to those capable of understanding.

A person who sees the letters in a beautifully written book without being able to read them will praise the skill of the copyist because he admires the graceful shape of the letters, but the purpose and meaning of these letters he does not grasp. What he sees with his eyes prompts him to praise, but his mind is not enriched with knowledge. Another, praising the artistry, will also grasp the meaning; one, that is, who is able not only to see what everyone else sees but also to read it, which is a skill that has to be learned. So too, those who observed Christ's miracles without grasping their purpose and the meaning they had for those able to understand, simply admired the deeds. Others went further: they admired the deeds and also grasped the meaning. As pupils in the school of Christ, we must be such as these.

(Sermon 98, 1-3: PL 38, 591-592)

Augustine (354-430) was born at Thagaste in Africa and received a Christian education, although he was not baptized until 387. In 391 he was ordained priest and in 395 he became coadjutor bishop to Valerius of Hippo, whom he succeeded in 396. Augustine's theology was formulated in the course of his struggle with three heresies: Manicheism, Donatism, and Pelagianism. His writings are voluminous and his influence on subsequent theology immense. He molded the thought of the Middle Ages down to the thirteenth century. Yet he was above all a pastor and a great spiritual writer.

Eleventh Sunday
in Ordinary Time

Gospel: Luke 7:36—8:3 or 7:36-50

Her many sins were forgiven her, because she has shown great love.

Commentary: Anonymous Syrian Writer

A sinful woman has proclaimed to us that God's love has gone forth in search of sinners. For when he called her, Christ was inviting our whole race to love; and in her person he was drawing all sinners to his forgiveness. He spoke to her alone, but he was drawing all creation to his grace. No one else persuaded him to help her come to forgiveness; only his love for the one he himself had formed persuaded him to do this, and his own grace besought him on behalf of the work of his hands.

Who would not be struck by the mercy of Christ, who accepted an invitation to a Pharisee's house in order to save a sinner! For the sake of the woman who hungered for forgiveness, he himself felt hunger for the table of Simon the Pharisee; and all the while, under the guise of a meal of bread, he had prepared for the sinner a meal of repentance!

The shepherd came down from heaven for the lost sheep, to catch in Simon's house the woman the cunning wolf had carried off. In the house of Simon the Pharisee he found the one he sought.

Seeing Jesus' feet, the sinner took them to be a symbol of his incarnation, and in grasping them believed herself to be grasping her God on the level of his corporal nature. By her words she besought him as her Creator—for clearly her words, though not written down, may be guessed at from her actions. She must surely have uttered words corresponding to her deeds when she bathed his feet with her tears, wiped them with her hair, and poured precious ointment over them. It was a prayer that she offered to the incarnate God: by bringing him her humility she showed her trust in him, and by the conversation they had with one another she proved him to be truly man.

Such then were the words addressed to Jesus by the sinner when she clasped his feet. He listened to them patiently, his silence proclaiming his steadfastness, his patience proclaiming his endurance. By his kindness he showed his approval of her boldness. He made it obvious that it was right for her to wrest pardon from him in the presence of all the guests. He did not speak at once and when he spoke he uttered only one word, but by that word he destroyed sins, abolished faults, chased away iniquity, granted pardon, uprooted evil, and made righteousness bud. All at once his forgiveness appeared within her soul and chased out of it the darkness of sin; she was cured, she recovered her wits, and gained both health and strength. For when Jesus gives graces he gives them lavishly, as he easily can, being the God of all things.

In order that you may have the same experience, reflect within yourself that your sin is great, but that it is blasphemy against God and damage to yourself to despair of his forgiveness because your sin seems to you to be too great. He has promised to forgive your sins, however many they are; will you tell him you cannot believe this and dispute with him, saying that your sin is too great; he cannot heal your sickness? Stop at this point, and cry out with the prophet, *Lord, I have sinned against you.* At once he will reply, "As for me, I have overlooked your fault: you shall not die." Glory to him from all of us, for all the ages. Amen.

(*Orient Syrien 7 [1962], 180-181.189.193.194*)

Twelfth Sunday
in Ordinary Time

Gospel: Luke 9:18-24

You are God's anointed one.

Commentary: Cyril of Alexandria

One day when Jesus was praying alone with his disciples he asked *them: "Who do the crowds say that I am?"* By praying alone accompanied only by his disciples the Lord and Savior of the world was setting them an example of a life befitting saints. However, there was a danger that this might disturb them and give them mistaken ideas. When they saw praying like a human being one whom the day before they had seen working miracles like God, they might well say among themselves: "This is very strange—who are we to think he is, God or a man?"

To put an end to any such mental turmoil and steady their unsettled faith, Jesus questioned them. He was not ignorant of what was being said of him by those outside the synagogue of the Jews or by the Israelites themselves, but he wanted to withdraw his disciples from the thinking of the multitude and establish right belief in them. *Who do the crowds say I am?* he asked.

Then Peter burst out before the rest and became the spokesman for the whole group, his words full of the love of God giving expression to a faith in Jesus which was correct and beyond reproach. *The Anointed of God*, he said. The disciple had weighed his words carefully and spoke of holy things with complete understanding. He did not say simply that Jesus was one anointed by God, but rather that he was *The Anointed.* For many were called anointed ones because God had anointed them in various ways, some as kings, some as prophets. Others like ourselves are called anointed ones because we have been saved by this Anointed One, the Savior of all the world, and have received the anointing of the Holy Spirit. Yes, many have received an anointing, and are therefore called anointed ones, but there is only One who is the Anointed of God the Father.

When the disciple had made his profession of faith Jesus *gave them strict orders to tell this to no one. "The Son of Man" he said, "must suffer greatly, and be rejected and killed, and raised up on the third day."*

Yet why was it not rather their duty to preach him everywhere? Surely this was the task of those who had been consecrated by him as apostles. However, as holy scripture says, *Every work has its own time.* Preaching Jesus had to follow events which had not yet taken place, namely, the crucifixion, the passion, the physical death, and the resurrection from the dead—that great and truly glorious miracle by which Emmanuel was attested as true God and by nature the Son of God the Father.

Jesus therefore commanded that the mystery should be honored by silence for the time being, until God's saving dispensation was brought to its proper conclusion. Then, when he had risen from the dead, he gave orders for it to be revealed to the whole world, and for all to be offered justification through faith and purification through holy baptism. *All authority in heaven and on earth has been given to me,* he said. *Go, therefore, and teach all nations. Baptize them in the name of the Father and of the Son and of the Holy Spirit, and instruct them to observe all the commandments I have given you. And remember that I am with you always, till the end of the world.*

> *(On Luke's Gospel 49: Edit. R.M. Tonneau,*
> *CSCO Script. Syri 70, 110-115)*

Cyril of Alexandria (d.444) succeeded his uncle Theophilus as patriarch in 412. Until 428 the pen of this brilliant theologian was employed in exegesis and polemics against the Arians; after that date it was devoted almost entirely to refuting the Nestorian heresy. The teaching of Nestorius was condemned in 431 by the Council of Ephesus at which Cyril presided, and Mary's title, Mother of God, was solemnly recognized. The incarnation is central to Cyril's theology. Only if Christ is consubstantial with the Father and with us can he save us, for the meeting ground between God and ourselves is the flesh of Christ. Through our kinship with Christ, the Word made flesh, we become children of God, and share in the filial relation of the Son with the Father.

Thirteenth Sunday in Ordinary Time

Gospel: Luke 9:51-62

Jesus resolutely took the road for Jerusalem.

Commentary: Hilary of Poitiers

Sure of protection on the day of battle, Christ prayed: *Lord, do not allow the wicked anything contrary to my desire.* He who said *I have come not to do my own will, but the will of him who sent me* hastened to fulfill the task he had undertaken out of obedience, though in such a way as to remind us that he possessed a will of his own. In fact, he willed whatever the Father willed. His saying *I have come not to do my own will, but the will of him who sent me* revealed who had sent him and whom he obeyed, but without detriment to his own power of willing.

Desiring to do everything the Father desired, Christ hastened to carry out his wishes with regard to his passion before the wicked could hinder him or prevent his doing so. He had a great longing to eat the passover with his disciples, and he celebrated the paschal meal in haste. He had an intense desire to drink the cup of his passion, for he said: *Shall I not drink the cup which my Father has given me?* When the search party came to arrest him and asked which man was Jesus, he stepped forward of his own accord. He asked for the sour wine which he knew he was destined to drink, and having drunk it and achieved his great purpose he said: *It is accomplished,* thus expressing his joy at obtaining his heart's desire.

In the psalms Christ had often prayed for his life to be delivered from the sword. He had shown in advance that not one of his bones was to be broken, and he had prophesied that his tunic was to be acquired by lot. He prayed that all these things willed by himself might come to pass so that prophecy might be fulfilled: that the wicked should have no control over them, that sinners should not hinder the celebration of that passover for which he so ardently longed, that fear should not stop them from presenting him with the cup of his passion—for those who came to arrest him all fell to the ground at the Lord's first reply to them. He prayed that the sour wine that was to be offered him might be ready, that the soldier's lance might not pierce his side before he had given up his spirit, and that no pretext for breaking his bones should be given by his slowness in dying. He prayed that no prophecy should be unfulfilled, and that nothing should be allowed the wicked contrary to his desire, but that everything not only prophesied but also willed by himself should be accomplished. He prayed about these things not because there was any danger of their not being accomplished, but so that everyone should perceive that the prophecies referred to himself.

(Commentary on the Psalms 39, 12: CSEL 22, 784-785)

Hilary (315-367) was elected bishop of Poitiers in 353. Because of his struggles with the Arians and his treatise on the Trinity, for which he was exiled, he has been called "the Athanasius of the West." He also wrote a commentary on Saint Matthew's gospel and another on a selection of the psalms. His style is difficult and obscure and he makes much use of allegory.

Fourteenth Sunday
in Ordinary Time

Gospel: Luke 10:1-12.17-20 or 10:1-9

Your peace will rest upon him.

Commentary: Augustine of Hippo

The gospel which has just been read raises a question. When the Lord told his disciples that the harvest was indeed abundant but laborers were scarce and urged them to ask the Lord of the harvest to send laborers out to harvest his crop, which crop did he have in mind? That was the point at which he increased the group of twelve disciples whom he had named his apostles by the addition of another seventy-two, and his words make it clear that he sent all these out to gather in the ripe grain.

But which crop did he mean? Evidently not a crop of Gentiles, from whom there was nothing to be reaped because there had as yet been no sowing among them. The conclusion must be that the crop in question consisted of Jews. The Jewish people were the harvest to which the Lord of the harvest came, and to which he dispatched his reapers. To the Gentiles he could send no reapers at that time, only sowers. We may understand, then, that harvest time among the Jews coincided with sowing time among the Gentiles, for out of the Jewish crop, sown by the prophets and now ripe for harvesting, the apostles were chosen.

Here we have the joy of observing the divine husbandry. How good it is to see God's gifts and watch the laborers in his field! Consider his twofold harvest, the one already reaped, the other still to come. That of the Jews is over and done, but there is a crop yet to be gathered in from the Gentiles.

Now let us see if this can be demonstrated. And what better place to look for evidence than the holy scriptures of the divine Lord of the harvest? Here in this very chapter of the gospel we have the saying: *The harvest is rich but the laborers are few; ask the Lord of the harvest to send laborers into his harvest.* This harvest is the people to whom the prophets preached, sowing the seed so that the apostles might gather in the sheaves. For the seed to sprout it was sufficient for the prophets to sow, but the ripe grain had to wait for the apostles' sickle.

Another time the Lord told his disciples: *You say that summer is still far off. Lift up your eyes and see that the fields are already white with ripe grain!* And he added: *Others have toiled over it, and you have entered into their labors.* Those others were Abraham, Isaac, Jacob, Moses, and the prophets. Because they worked hard at sowing, at the Lord's coming the grain was found to be ripe. Then the reapers were sent out, wielding the gospel as their sickle. They were to greet no one on the road, which meant they were to have no aim or activity apart from proclaiming the Good News in a spirit of brotherly love. When they arrived at a house they were to say: *Peace be to this house.* This greeting was no mere formula; being filled with peace themselves, the apostles spread it abroad, proclaiming peace and at the same time possessing it. Consequently when one of them, fully at peace with himself, pronounced the blessing: *Peace be to this house,* then if a lover of peace were in that house, the apostle's peace would rest upon him.

(Sermon 101, 1-3.11: PL 38, 605-607.610)

Augustine (354-430) was born at Thagaste in Africa and received a Christian education, although he was not baptized until 387. In 391 he was ordained priest and in 395 he became coadjutor bishop to Valerius of Hippo, whom he succeeded in 396. Augustine's theology was formulated in the course of his struggle with three heresies: Manicheism, Donatism, and Pelagianism. His writings are voluminous and his influence on subsequent theology immense. He molded the thought of the Middle Ages down to the thirteenth century. Yet he was above all a pastor and a great spiritual writer.

Fifteenth Sunday in Ordinary Time

Gospel: Luke 10:25-37

Who is my neighbor?

Commentary: Origen of Alexandria

To interpret the parable of the Good Samaritan, one of the elders used to say that the man going down from Jerusalem to Jericho was Adam. He said Jerusalem was paradise, Jericho was the world, and the brigands were enemy powers. The priest was the law, the Levite the prophets, and the Samaritan Christ. Adam's wounds were his disobedience, the animal that carried him was the body of the Lord, and the "pandochium" or inn, open to all who wished to enter, was the Church. The two denarii represented the Father and the Son, and the innkeeper was the head of the Church, who was entrusted with its administration. The promised return of the Samaritan was a figure of the second coming of the Savior.

The Samaritan was carrying oil—*oil to make his face shine* as scripture says, referring surely to the face of the man he cared for. He cleansed the man's wounds with oil to soothe the inflammation and with wine that made them smart, and then placed him on his own mount, that is, on his own body, since he had condescended to assume our humanity. This Samaritan bore our sins and suffered on our behalf; he carried the half dead man to the inn which takes in everyone, denying no one its help; in other words, to the Church. To this inn Jesus invites all when he says: *Come to me, all who labor and are overburdened, and I will give you new strength.*

After bringing in the man half dead the Samaritan did not immediately depart, but remained and dressed his wounds by night as well as by day, showing his concern and doing everything he could for him. In the morning when he wished to set out again he took from his own pure silver coins, from his own sterling money, two denarii to pay the innkeeper—clearly the angel of the Church—and ordered him to nurse with all diligence and restore to health the man whom for a short time he himself had personally tended.

I think the two denarii stand for knowledge of the Father and the Son in the Father. This was given to the angel as a recompense, so that he would care more diligently for the man entrusted to him. He was also promised that whatever he spent of his own in healing him would be repaid.

This guardian of souls *who showed mercy to the man who fell into the hands of brigands* was a better neighbor to him than were either the law or the prophets, and he proved this more by deeds than by words. Now the saying: *Be imitators of me as I am of Christ* makes it clear that we can imitate Christ by showing mercy to those who have fallen into the hands of brigands. We can go to them, bandage their wounds after pouring in oil and wine, place them on our own mount, and bear their burdens. And so the Son of God exhorts us to do these things, in words addressed not only to the teacher of the law but to all of us: *Go and do likewise.* If we do, we shall gain eternal life in Christ Jesus, *to whom belongs glory and power for ever and ever. Amen.*

(*On Luke's Gospel 34, 3.7-9: SC 87, 402-410*)

Origen (183-253), one of the greatest thinkers of ancient times, became head of the catechetical school of Alexandria at the age of eighteen. In 230 he was ordained priest by the bishop of Caesarea. His life was entirely devoted to the study of scripture and he was also a great master of the spiritual life. His book *On First Principles* was the first great theological synthesis. Many of his works are extant only in Latin as a result of his posthumous condemnation for heterodox teaching. Nevertheless, in intention he was always a loyal son of the Church.

Sixteenth Sunday in Ordinary Time

Gospel: Luke 10:38-42

Martha welcomed Jesus into her house. Mary has chosen the better part.

Commentary: Bruno of Segni

Everything our Savior did was full of sacred teaching. In every situation his actions were meant to point beyond themselves. For example, his outward actions in the hillside village of Bethany are repeated every day in his holy church. Daily the Lord Jesus enters in, not thinking frequent visits beneath his dignity. There he is welcomed by Martha, who takes him into her home.

Let us see then what Martha stands for, and what Mary symbolizes. Each of them denotes something important, for these two make up the entire Church.

One of them, namely Martha, symbolizes the active life; the other, Mary, the contemplative. That is why scripture says it was Martha, not Mary, who received Christ into her house. Mary, of course, does not own a house, since the contemplative life entails the renunciation of all worldly possessions. All that contemplatives want to do is to sit at the feet of the Lord—to read, pray, and give themselves up to contemplating God is their whole desire. It is enough for them to be always listening to the word of God and feeding their minds rather than their stomachs. Such as these were the apostles and prophets; such are many others who, leaving everything, flee from the world and cling to the Lord. They seem to possess nothing, yet they have everything. Only good people can live this kind of life, whereas both good and bad alike can lead active lives.

Now the reason the active life is so called is because it consists of constant activity, weariness, and toil, so that scarcely a moment's quiet can be found in it. We are not referring here though to that kind of active life that occupies thieves, impels tyrants, tempts misers, stirs up adulterers, and incites all wicked people to commit evil deeds. For just as we speak only of one Martha who was Mary's sister, so we are referring only to that type of active life which is most closely related to the contemplative life, that is, an active life that is pure and blameless.

When the apostle preached and baptized, worked with his hands to gain a livelihood, journeyed from city to city, and showed solicitude for all the churches, was he not living the active life? In the same way then our text says of Martha that she was *busy with much serving.* In fact, right down to the present day we see prelates in charge of the churches and the other clergy devotedly hurrying to and fro about their work, hot and bothered, sweating over the needs of their brothers and sisters in various ways, so that we may rightly describe them also as *busy with much serving.* The contemplative life then is superior to the active because it is free from anxiety and will never end. Nevertheless the active life is so indispensable that in this world the contemplative life itself cannot exist without it.

(On Luke's Gospel 1, 10: PL 165, 390-391)

Bruno of Segni (d.1123) was born near Asti in Piedmont, and studied at the university of Bologna before being made a canon of Siena. At the Council of Rome (1079) he defended the Catholic doctrine of the eucharist against Berengarius. In the following year Gregory VII, his personal friend, made him bishop of Segni, but he refused a cardinalate. Bruno was a zealous pastor, and shared in all the projects of Gregory VII for the reform of the Church. In his writings he attacked simony and lay investiture. He was the greatest scripture commentator of his age. Longing for solitude, he received the monastic habit at Monte Cassino and in 1107 became abbot, but was later ordered by Pope Paschal II to return to his see.

Seventeenth Sunday
in Ordinary Time

Gospel: Luke 11:1-13

Ask, and it will be given to you.

Commentary: Venerable Bede

Our Lord and Savior wishes us to attain the joy of the heavenly kingdom, and so he taught us to pray for it, promising to give it to us if we did so. *Ask,* he said, *and you will receive, seek and you will find, knock and the door will be opened to you.*

We should consider most seriously and attentively what these words of the Lord may mean for us, for they warn that not the idle and feckless but those who ask, seek, and knock will receive, find, and have the door opened to them. We must therefore ask for entry into the kingdom by prayer, seek it by upright living, and knock at its door by perseverance. Merely to ask verbally is not enough; we must also diligently seek to discover how to live so as to be worthy of obtaining what we ask for. We know this from our Savior's words: *Not everyone who says to me, "Lord, Lord" will enter the kingdom of heaven, but only those who do the will of my heavenly Father.*

There is a need, then, for constant and unflagging prayer. Let us fall upon our knees with tears before our God and Maker; and that we may deserve a hearing, let us consider carefully how he who made us wishes us to live, and what he has commanded us to do. *Let us seek the Lord and his strength; let us constantly seek his face.* And in order to become worthy of finding him and gazing upon him, *let us cleanse ourselves from all defilement of body and spirit,* for only the chaste of body can be raised up to heaven on the day of resurrection; only the pure of heart can contemplate the glory of the divine Majesty.

If we would know what the Lord wishes us to ask for, let us listen to the gospel text: *Seek first the kingdom of God and its justice, and all these other things will be given you as well.* To seek the kingdom of God and its justice is to long for the graces of our heavenly homeland, and to give constant thought to the kind of upright living that will deserve to obtain them; for should we chance to stray from the path that leads there we shall never be able to reach our goal.

To ask God for the justice of his kingdom is to ask principally for faith, hope, and love. These virtues above all we should strive to obtain, for scripture says: *The upright live by faith; mercy surrounds those who hope in the Lord;* and *To love is to fulfill the law, for the whole law is summed up in one word: You shall love your neighbor as yourself.* And so the Lord graciously promises that *the Father will give the good Spirit to those who ask him,* in order to show that those who of themselves are evil can become good by receiving the grace of the Spirit. He promises the good Spirit will be given by the Father because whether it is faith, hope, or any other virtue we desire to obtain, we shall do so only through the grace of the Holy Spirit.

As we do our best, then, to follow in our Lord's footsteps, let us ask God the Father for the grace of his Spirit to lead us along the path of that true faith which works through love. And that we may deserve to obtain our desire, let us strive to live in a way that will make us not unworthy of so great a Father; let us preserve inviolate in body and soul the sacramental rebirth of our baptism which made us children of God. Then, if we keep the almighty Father's commandments, he will certainly reward us with the eternal blessing which from the beginning he prepared as our heritage through Jesus Christ our Lord, who with the Holy spirit lives and reigns with him, God for ever and ever. Amen.

(Homily 14: CCL 122, 272-273.277-279)

Bede (c.673-735), who received the title of Venerable less than a century after his death, was placed at the age of seven in the monastery of Wearmouth, then ruled by Saint Benet Biscop. At the age of 30 he was ordained priest. His whole life was devoted to the study of scripture, to teaching, writing, and the prayer of the Divine Office. He was famous for his learning, although he never went beyond the bounds of his native Northumbria. Bede is best known for his historical works, which earned him the title "Father of English History." His *Historia Ecclesiastica Gentis Anglorum* is a primary source for early English history, especially valuable because of the care he took to give his authorities, and to separate historical fact from hearsay and tradition.

Eighteenth Sunday in Ordinary Time

Gospel: Luke 12:13-21

What am I to do? I have not enough room to store my crops.

Commentary: Basil the Great

The land of a rich man produced abundant harvests, and he thought to himself: "What am I to do? I will pull down my barns, and build larger ones."

Now why did that land bear so well, when it belonged to a man who would make no good use of its fertility? It was to show more clearly the forbearance of God, whose kindness extends even to such people as this. *He sends rain on both the just and the unjust, and makes the sun rise on the wicked and the good alike.*

But what do we find in this man? A bitter disposition, hatred of other people, unwillingness to give. This is the return he made to his Benefactor. He forgot that we all share the same nature; he felt no obligation to distribute his surplus to the needy. His barns were full to bursting point, but still his miserly heart was not satisfied. Year by year he increased his wealth, always adding new crops to the old. The result was a hopeless impasse: greed would not permit him to part with anything he possessed, and yet because he had so much there was no place to store his latest harvest. And so he was incapable of making a decision and could find no escape from his anxiety. *What am I to do?*

Who would not pity a man so oppressed? His land yields him no profit but only sighs; it brings him no rich returns but only cares and distress and a terrible helplessness. He laments in the same way as the poor do. Is not his cry like that of one hard pressed by poverty? *What am I to do?* How can I find food and clothing?

You who have wealth, recognize who has given you the gifts you have received. Consider yourself, who you are, what has been committed to your charge, from whom you have received it, why you have been preferred to most other people. You are the servant of the good God, a steward on behalf of your fellow servants. Do not imagine that everything has been provided for your own stomach. Take decisions regarding your property as though it belonged to another. Possessions give you pleasure for a short time, but then they will slip through your fingers and be gone, and you will be required to give an exact account of them.

What am I to do? It would have been so easy to say: "I will feed the hungry, I will open my barns and call in all the poor. I will imitate Joseph in proclaiming my good will toward everyone. I will issue the generous invitation: 'Let anyone who lacks bread come to me. You shall share, each according to need, in the good things God has given me, just as though you were drawing from a common well'."

(Homilies on Riches, Courtonne, pages 15-19)

Basil the Great (c.330-379), one of the three great Cappadocian Fathers, received an excellent education and began a career as a rhetorician before a spiritual awakening led him to receive baptism and become a monk. After visiting ascetics in Egypt, Palestine, Syria, and Mesopotamia, he decided that it was better for monks to live together in monasteries than alone as hermits, and he set about organizing Cappadocian monasticism. Basil's Rules influenced Saint Benedict. In 370 Basil succeeded Eusebius as bishop of Caesarea. His main concern was for the unity of the Church, and he strove to establish better relations between Rome and the East. His efforts bore fruit only after his death. Basil's writings include dogmatic, ascetic, and pedagogic treatises as well as letters and sermons.

Nineteenth Sunday
in Ordinary Time

Gospel: Luke 12:32-48

See that you are prepared.

Commentary: Gregory of Nyssa

When the Lord says: *Let your loins be girded and your lamps lit,* he is warning us to stay awake; for a light shining in one's eyes drives away sleep, and a tightly-fastened belt also makes sleep difficult, as the discomfort prevents relaxation. But the real meaning of the parable is perfectly clear: a person girded with temperance lives in the light of a clear conscience before God. And so, with the light of truth shining, the soul stays awake and is not deceived. It does not dally with illusive dreams.

If following the guidance of the Word we attain this goal, our lives will in a way be like those of the angels, for we are compared with them in the divine command: *You must be like people waiting for their master to return from a wedding, ready to open the door immediately when he comes and knocks.* It was the angels who were awaiting the Master's return from the wedding. They sat with unsleeping eyes at the heavenly gates, so that when he returned the King of glory might pass through them once more into the heavenly bliss from which, as the psalm says, he had come forth like a bridegroom from his tent. He took us to himself as his virgin bride, our nature once prostituted to idols being restored by sacramental rebirth to virginal incorruptibility. After the marriage, when the Church had been wedded to the Word— as John says, *He who has the bride is the bridegroom*—and admitted to the bridal chamber of the sacred mysteries, the angels awaited the King of glory's return to the blessedness which is his by nature.

And so the Lord said our lives should be like theirs. Just as they, living lives far removed from sin and error, are ready to receive the

Lord at his coming, so we also should keep watch at the entrance of our houses, and prepare ourselves to obey him when he comes to our door and knocks. *Blessed,* he says, *are those servants whom the master finds so doing when he comes.*

(On the Song of Songs 11: Jaeger VI, 317-319)

Gregory of Nyssa (c.330-395), the younger brother of Basil the Great, chose a secular career and married. Reluctantly, however, in 371, he received episcopal ordination and became bishop of Nyssa, an unimportant town in Basil's metropolitan district of Caesarea. Gregory was the greatest speculative theologian of the three Cappadocian Fathers, and the first after Origen to attempt a systematic presentation of the Christian faith. Gifted spiritually as well as intellectually, he has been called "the father of Christian mysticism." His spiritual interpretation of scripture shows the influence of Origen.

Twentieth Sunday
in Ordinary Time

Gospel: Luke 12:49-53

I have come not to bring peace, but division.

Commentary: Denis the Carthusian

I have come to cast fire upon the earth. In other words, I have come down from the highest heaven and appeared to men and women through the mystery of the incarnation in order to light the fire of divine love in human hearts. *And how I wish it were already ablaze!* How I wish it were already kindled, fanned into flame by the Holy Spirit, and leaping forth in good works.

Christ foretells that he will suffer death on a cross before the human race is inflamed by the fire of this love; for it was by his most holy passion that he won so great a gift for humankind, and it is chiefly the recollection of his passion that kindles the flame of love in Christian hearts.

There is a baptism which I must undergo. By divine decree there remains for me the duty of receiving a baptism of blood, that is, of being bathed, soaked upon the cross not in water but in my own blood poured out to redeem the whole world. *And what constraint I am under until that has been achieved*—until my passion is love and I say: *It is accomplished.* For Christ was impelled incessantly by the love within him.

The way to attain the perfection of divine love is then stated. *Do you think that I have come to bring peace on earth?* In other words: Do not imagine that I have come to offer people a sensual, worldly, and unruly peace that will enable them to be united in their vices and achieve earthly prosperity. *No, I tell you,* I have not come to offer that kind of peace, *but rather division*—a good, healthy kind of division, physical as well as spiritual. Love for God and desire for inner peace will set those who believe in me at odds with wicked men and women, and make them part company with those who would turn them from their course of spiritual progress and from the purity of divine love, or who attempt to hinder them.

Good, interior, spiritual peace consists in the repose of the mind in God, and in a rightly ordered harmony. To bestow this peace was the chief reason for Christ's coming. This inner peace flows from love. It is an unassailable joy of the mind in God, and it is called peace of heart. It is the beginning and a kind of foretaste of the peace of the saints in heaven—the peace of eternity.

(On Luke's Gospel: Opera omnia XII, 72-74)

Denis the Carthusian (1408-1471), whose family name was van Leeuwen, was educated at Cologne and entered the Charterhouse at Roermund in 1423. His biblical commentaries cover both Old and New Testaments. He was strongly influenced by the writings of Pseudo-Denis and was himself a mystic: he was afterwards to be known as "Doctor Ecstaticus." He also took a practical interest in ecclesiastical discipline and in 1451 accompanied Nicholas of Cusa on a mission of Church reform and preached a crusade with him.

Twenty-First Sunday in Ordinary Time

Gospel: Luke 13:22-30

People from the east and from the west will come to take their place in the kingdom of God.

Commentary: Anselm of Canterbury

God cries out that the kingdom of heaven is for sale. The glorious bliss of this kingdom surpasses the power of mortal eye to see, mortal ear to hear, mortal heart to conceive. If anyone asks the price that must be paid, the answer is: The One who wishes to bestow a kingdom in heaven has no need of earthly payment. No one can give God anything he does not possess, because everything belongs to him. Yet he does not give such a precious gift entirely gratis, for he will not give it to anyone who lacks love. After all, people do not give away what they hold dear to those without appreciation. So since God has no need of your possessions but must not bestow such a precious gift on anyone who disdains to value it, love is the one thing he asks for; without this he cannot give it. Give love, then, and receive the kingdom: love and it is yours.

To reign in heaven simply means exercising a single power with God and all the holy angels and saints through being so united with them in love as to want only what they want. Love God more than yourself, then, and already you will begin to have what you desire to possess fully in heaven. Be at one with God and with other men and women—so long as they are not at variance with God—and already you will begin to reign with God and all the saints. The desires of God and all the saints will be the same as yours in heaven, if your desires now are the same as those of God and other people. So, if you want to be a king in heaven, love God and other people as you should and then you will deserve to become what you desire.

But you cannot have this perfect love unless you empty your heart of every other love. That is why those who fill their hearts with love of God and neighbor desire nothing but the will of God or that of some fellow human being—provided this is not contrary to God. That is why they devote themselves to prayer, spiritual conversations, and reflection, for it is a joy to them to long for God and to speak, hear, and think about him whom they dearly love. That is why they rejoice with those who rejoice, weep with those who weep, show compassion to those in distress, and give to the needy, since they love others as themselves. Hence too their contempt for riches, power, pleasure, honor, and praise. Those who love these things frequently offend against God and their neighbor—for *the whole law and the prophets depend on these two commandments.* So those who wish to possess the fullness of that love which is the price of the kingdom of heaven should love contempt, poverty, toil, and subjection, as do the saints.

(Letter 112: Opera omnia, III, 244-246)

Anselm (c.1033-1109) was born at Aosta in Italy. In 1060, at the age of 27, he became a monk at Bec in Normandy, and three years later was elected abbot. In 1093 he succeeded Lanfranc as archbishop of Canterbury. Anselm made an outstanding contribution to the speculative thought of his day, and may properly be called the "Father of Scholasticism." His classic definition of theology as "faith seeking understanding" is still valid today.

Twenty-Second Sunday in Ordinary Time

Gospel: Luke 14:1.7-14

The one who exalts himself shall be humbled and the one who humbles himself shall be exalted.

Commentary: Bruno of Segni

Invited to a wedding feast, the Lord looked round and noticed how all were choosing the first and most honorable places, each person wanting to take precedence over the others and to be raised above them. He then told them this parable, which even taken literally is most useful and appropriate for all who like to be honored, and fear being put to shame. To those of lower station it accords courtesy, and to those of higher condition respect. However, since it is called a parable, it must have some other interpretation besides the literal one. Let us see then what this wedding feast is, and who are the people invited to it.

This wedding feast takes place in the Church every day. Every day the Lord makes a wedding feast, for every day he unites faithful souls to himself, some coming to be baptized, others leaving this world for the kingdom of heaven. We are all invited to this wedding feast—all of us who have received faith in Christ and the seal of baptism. This table set before us is that of which it is said: *You have prepared a table before me in the sight of those who trouble me.* Here is the showbread, here the fatted calf, here the lamb who takes away the sins of the world. Here is the living bread come down from heaven, here placed before us is the chalice of the New Covenant, here are the gospels and the letters of the apostles, here the books of Moses and the prophets. It is as though a dish containing every delight was brought and set before us. What more then can we desire? What reason is there for choosing the first seats? There is plenty for all no matter where we sit. There is nothing we shall lack.

But whoever you may be who still desire the first place here—go and sit in the last place. Do not be lifted up by pride, inflated by knowledge, elated by nobility, but the greater you are the more you must humble yourself in every way, and you will find grace with God. In his own time he will say to you: *Friend, go up higher, and then you will be honored by all who sit at table with you.* Moses sat in the last place whenever he had the choice. When the Lord wishing to send him to the Israelites, invited him to take a higher place, his answer was: *I beg you, Lord, send someone else. I am not a good speaker.* It was the same as saying: "I am not worthy of so great an office." Saul, too, was of small account in his own eyes when the Lord made him king. And Jeremiah, similarly, was afraid of rising to the first place: *Ah, Lord God,* he said, *look, I cannot speak—I am only a child.*

In the church, then, the first seat, or the highest place, is to be sought not by ambition but by humility; not by money but by holiness.

(On Luke's Gospel II, 14: PL 165, 406-407)

Bruno of Segni (d.1123) was born near Asti in Piedmont, and studied at the university of Bologna before being made a canon of Siena. At the Council of Rome (1079) he defended the Catholic doctrine of the eucharist against Berengarius. In the following year Gregory VII, his personal friend, made him bishop of Segni, but he refused a cardinalate. Bruno was a zealous pastor, and shared in all the projects of Gregory VII for the reform of the Church. In his writings he attacked simony and lay investiture. He was the greatest scripture commentator of his age. Longing for solitude, he received the monastic habit at Monte Cassino and in 1107 became abbot, but was later ordered by Pope Paschal II to return to his see.

Twenty-Third Sunday in Ordinary Time

Gospel: Luke 14:25-33

The person who does not renounce his possessions cannot be my disciple.

Commentary: John Cassian

The tradition of the Fathers and the authority of holy scripture both affirm that there are three renunciations which every one of us must strive to practice. To these let us turn our attention.

First, on the material level, we have to despise all worldly wealth and possessions; secondly, we must reject our former way of life with its vices and attachments, both physical and spiritual; and thirdly, we should withdraw our mind from all that is transitory and visible to contemplate solely what lies in the future and to desire what is unseen.

We read that the Lord commanded Abraham to make all three renunciations at once when he said to him: *Leave your country and your kindred and your father's house.* First he said *your country,* meaning worldly wealth and possessions; secondly *your kindred,* that is our former way of living, with its habits and vices which have grown up with us and are as familiar to us as kith and kin; thirdly *your father's house,* in other words every secular memory aroused by what we see.

This forgetfulness will be achieved when, dead with Christ to the elemental spirits of this world, we contemplate as the apostle says, *not the things that are seen but those that are unseen, for what is seen is temporal but what is unseen is eternal.* It will be achieved when in our hearts we leave this temporal and visible house and turn the eyes of our mind toward that in which we shall live for ever; when, though living in the world, we cease to follow the spirit of the world in order to fight for the Lord, proclaiming by our holy way of life that, as the apostle says, *our homeland is in heaven.*

It avails little to undertake the first of these renunciations, even with wholehearted devotion inspired by faith, unless we carry out the second with the same zeal and fervor. Then having accomplished this as well we shall be able to go on to the third, whereby we leave the house of our former father, of him who fathered us as members of a fallen race, *children of wrath like everyone else,* and turn our inward gaze solely toward heavenly things.

We shall attain to the perfection of this third renunciation when our mind, no longer dulled by contact with a pampered body, has been cleansed by the most searching refinement from every worldly sentiment and attitude, and raised by constant meditation on divine things and spiritual contemplation to the realm of the invisible. It will then lose all awareness of the frail body enclosing it or of the place it occupies, so absorbed will it be by things divine and spiritual.

(Conference 3, 6-7: SC 42, 145-147)

John Cassian (c.360-435) is renowned for having introduced knowledge of Eastern monasticism into the West, thus influencing the development of ascetic spirituality. After his initiation into monastic life at Bethlehem, he spent fourteen years in the Egyptian desert imbibing the wisdom of the Fathers. He was ordained deacon at Constantinople by Saint John Chrysostom, was sent on an embassy to Rome, and finally settled at Marseilles, where he founded two monasteries. His outstanding works on the monastic life are the Institutes and Conferences. He entered into controversy with Saint Augustine on the subject of grace and free will, but the exchange was marked by mutual respect. Cassian laid great stress on the need for effort in the ascetical life, but that grace is always presupposed is shown by the enormous importance he attached to prayer. The label of semi-pelagian later attached to his name is therefore undeserved.

Twenty-Fourth Sunday in Ordinary Time

Gospel: Luke 15:1-32 or 15:1-10

There will be joy in heaven over one sinner who repents.

Commentary: Peter Chrysologus

Finding something we have lost gives us a fresh joy, and we are happier at having found the lost object than we should have been had we never lost it. This parable, however, is concerned more with divine tenderness and compassion than with human behavior, and it expresses a great truth. Humans are too greedy to forsake things of value for love of anything inferior. That is something only God can do. For God not only brought what was not into being, but he also went after what was lost while still protecting what he left behind, and found what was lost without losing what he had in safe keeping.

This story, then, speaks of no earthly shepherd but of a heavenly one, and far from being a portrayal of human activity, this whole parable conceals divine mysteries, as becomes clear from the number mentioned when Christ says: *Which of you, if you have a hundred sheep and lost one of them...* You see how the loss of a single sheep made the shepherd grieve as though the whole flock were no longer in safe keeping but had gone astray, and how this made him leave the ninety-nine to go after the lost one and search for it, so that its recovery might make the flock complete again.

But let us now unfold the hidden meaning of this heavenly parable. The man who owns the hundred sheep is Christ. He is the good shepherd, the loving shepherd, who in a single sheep, that is in Adam, fashioned the whole flock of humankind. He set this sheep in a place of rich pasturage amidst the pleasures of paradise, but heedless of the shepherd's voice it trusted in the howling of wolves, lost the protection of the sheepfold, and was pierced through by deadly wounds.

Christ therefore came into the world to look for it, and he found it in the Virgin's womb. He came in the body assumed at his human birth, and raising that body on the cross, he placed the lost sheep on his own shoulders by his passion. Then in the intense joy of the resurrection he brought it to its heavenly home. *And he called his friends and neighbors,* that is the angels, and said to them: *Rejoice with me, for I have found the sheep that was lost.*

The angels joined Christ in gladness and rejoicing at the return of the Lord's sheep. They did not take it amiss that he now reigned over them upon the throne of majesty, for the sin of envy had long since been banished from heaven together with the devil, and it could not gain entry there again through the Lamb who took away the sin of the world!

Brothers and sisters, Christ sought us on earth; let us seek him in heaven. He has borne us up to the glory of his divinity; let us bear him in our bodies by holiness. As the apostle says: *Glorify and bear God in your bodies.* That person bears God in his body whose bodily activities are free from sin.

(Homily 168: PL 52, 639-641)

Peter Chrysologus (c.400-450), who was born at Imola in Italy, became a bishop of Ravenna. He was highly esteemed by the Empress Galla Placidia, in whose presence he preached his first sermon as bishop. He was above all a pastor, and many of his sermons have been preserved.

Twenty-Fifth Sunday in Ordinary Time

Gospel: Luke 16:1-13

You cannot be the slave both of God and of money.

Commentary: Gaudentius of Brescia

The Lord Jesus, true teacher of the precepts that lead to salvation, wished to urge upon the apostles in his own time and all believers today the Christian duty of almsgiving. He therefore related the parable of the steward to make us realize that nothing in this world really belongs to us. We have been entrusted with the administration of our Lord's property to use what we need with thanksgiving, and to distribute the rest among our fellow servants according to the needs of each one. We must not squander the wealth entrusted to us, nor use it on superfluities, for when the Lord comes we shall be required to account for our expenditure.

Finally, at the end of the parable, the Lord adds: *Use worldly wealth to make friends with the poor, so that when it fails you,* when you have spent all you possessed on the needs of the poor and have nothing left, *they may welcome you into eternal dwellings.*

In other words, these same poor people will befriend you by assuring your salvation, for Christ, the giver of eternal rewards, will declare that he himself received the acts of kindness done to them. Not in their own name, then, will these poor folk welcome us, but in the name of him who is refreshed in their persons by the fruit of our faith and obedience. Those who exercised this ministry of love will be received into the eternal dwellings of the kingdom of heaven, for the King will say: *Come, blessed of my Father, take possession of the kingdom prepared for you from the beginning of the world; for I was hungry and you fed me, thirsty and you gave me a drink.*

But *if you have been untrustworthy in the administration of worldly wealth, who is going to trust you with true riches?* For if someone cannot be relied on to administer worldly possessions that provide the means for all sorts of wrong doing, would anyone dream of trusting that person with the true heavenly riches rightly and deservedly enjoyed by those who have been faithful in giving to the poor?

The Lord's query above is immediately followed by another: *If you cannot be trusted with another's property, who will give you your own?* Nothing in this world really belongs to us. We who hope for a future reward are told to live in this world as strangers and pilgrims, so as to be able to say to the Lord without fear of contradiction: *I am a stranger and a pilgrim like all my ancestors.*

What believers can regard as their own is that eternal and heavenly possession where our heart is and our treasure, and where intense longing makes us dwell already through faith, for as Saint Paul teaches, *Our homeland is in heaven.*

(Sermon 18: PL 20, 973-975)

Gaudentius of Brescia (+410) became bishop in succession to Saint Philaster sometime before 397, and governed his church for fourteen years. He was a friend of Saint Ambrose and of Saint John Chrysostom. In 404-405 he pleaded Chrysostom's cause at Constantinople as the envoy of Pope Innocent I. The sermons of Gaudentius were known and used by Saint Leo the Great. They are important for their teaching on the eucharist.

Twenty-Sixth Sunday
in Ordinary Time

Gospel: Luke 16:19-31

During your life good things came your way just as bad things came the way of
Lazarus. Now he is being comforted while you are in agony.

Commentary: John Chrysostom

It is worthwhile inquiring why the rich man saw Lazarus in Abraham's arms, and not in the company of some other righteous person.
The reason is that Abraham was hospitable, and so the sight of Lazarus
with Abraham was meant to reproach the rich man for his own
inhospitality. Abraham used to pursue even passers-by and drag them
into his home, whereas the rich man disregarded someone lying in his
own doorway. Although he had within his grasp so great a treasure,
such an opportunity to win salvation, he ignored the poor man day
after day. He could have helped him but he failed to do so. The
patriarch was not like that but just the opposite. He would sit in his
doorway and catch all who passed by. And just as a fisherman casting
a net into the sea hauls up fish, yes, but also quite often gold and pearls,
so Abraham whilst catching people in his net finished by catching
angels, though strangely enough without knowing it.

Even Paul marvels at this and gives the advice: *Remember to
welcome strangers into your homes, for some by so doing have
entertained angels without knowing it.* And he did well to say *without
knowing it,* for if Abraham had welcomed his guests with such
kindness because he knew who they were he would have done nothing
remarkable. He is praiseworthy only because, without knowing who
the passers-by were and taking them to be simply human wayfarers,
he yet invited them in with so much good will.

And this is true of you also. If you show much eagerness in
welcoming some famous and distinguished person you do nothing

120

remarkable; often the high rank of a guest compels even a reluctant host to show every sign of courtesy. But we do something truly great and admirable when we give a most courteous welcome to all, even the outcasts of society or people of humble condition. Hence Christ himself praised those who so acted, declaring: *Whatever you did for one of these very poor people you did to me.* He also said: *It is not your Father's will that one of these little ones should perish.* Indeed, throughout the gospel Christ speaks a great deal about the little people and those of the humblest condition.

And so Abraham also, knowing this, did not ask who travelers were or where they came from, as we do today, but simply welcomed them all. Anyone wishing to show kindness should not inquire into other people's lives, but has only to alleviate their poverty and supply their needs, as Christ commanded when he said: *Imitate your Father in heaven, who makes his sun rise on good and bad alike, and sends rain on the just and the unjust.*

(Homily on Lazarus 2, 5: Bareille II, 582-583)

John Chrysostom (c.347-407) was born at Antioch and studied under Diodore of Tarsus, the leader of the Antiochene school of theology. After a period of great austerity as a hermit, he returned to Antioch where he was ordained deacon in 381 and priest in 386. From 386 to 397 it was his duty to preach in the principal church of the city, and his best homilies, which earned him the title "Chrysostomos" or "the golden-mouthed," were preached at this time. In 397 Chrysostom became patriarch of Constantinople, where his efforts to reform the court, clergy, and people led to his exile in 404 and finally to his death from the hardships imposed on him. Chrysostom stressed the divinity of Christ against the Arians and his full humanity against the Apollinarians, but he had no speculative bent. He was above all a pastor of souls, and was one of the most attractive personalities of the early Church.

Twenty-Seventh Sunday in Ordinary Time

Gospel: Luke 17:5-10

If you had faith!

Commentary: Augustine of Hippo

Reading the holy gospel nourishes in us the habit of prayer, builds up our faith, and disposes us to trust in the Lord rather than in ourselves. What more powerful incentive to prayer could be proposed to us than the parable of the unjust judge? An unprincipled man, without fear of God or regard for other people, that judge nevertheless ended by granting the widow's petition. No kindly sentiment moved him to do so; he was rather worn down by her pestering. Now if a man can grant a request even when it is odious to him to be asked, how can we be refused by the one who urges us to ask?

Having persuaded us, therefore, by a comparison of opposites that *we ought always to pray and never lose heart,* the Lord goes on to put the question: *Nevertheless, when the Son of Man comes, do you think he will find faith on earth?* Where there is no faith, there is no prayer. Who would pray for something he did not believe in? So when the blessed apostle exhorts us to pray he begins by declaring: *Whoever calls on the name of the Lord will be saved;* but to show that faith is the source of prayer and the stream will not flow if its springs are dried up, he continues: *But how can people call on him in whom they do not believe?*

We must believe, then, in order to pray; and we must ask God that the faith enabling us to pray may not fail. Faith gives rise to prayer, and this prayer obtains an increase of faith. Faith, I say, gives rise to prayer, and is in turn strengthened by prayer. It was to guard against their faith failing in times of temptation that the Lord told his disciples: *Watch and pray that you may not enter into temptation.*

Watch, he says; *and pray that you may not enter into temptation.* What does it mean to enter into temptation? It means to turn one's back on faith. Temptation grows stronger in proportion as faith weakens, and becomes weaker in proportion as faith grows strong. To convince you, beloved, that he was speaking of the weakening and loss of faith when he told his disciples to watch and pray that they might not enter into temptation, the Lord said in this same passage of the gospel: *This night Satan has demanded to sift you like wheat; but I have prayed for you, Peter, that your faith may not fail.* Is the protector to pray, while the person in danger has no need to do so?

But in asking whether the Son of Man would find faith on earth at his coming, the Lord was speaking of perfect faith. That kind of faith is indeed hardly to be found on earth. Look at God's Church: it is full of people. Who would come here if faith were non-existent? But who would not move mountains if that faith were present in full measure? Mark the apostles: they would never have left everything they possessed and spurned worldly ambition to follow the Lord unless their faith had been great; and yet that faith of theirs could not have been perfect, otherwise they would not have asked the Lord to increase it.

(Sermon 115: PL 38, 655)

Augustine (354-430) was born at Thagaste in Africa and received a Christian education, although he was not baptized until 387. In 391 he was ordained priest and in 395 he became coadjutor bishop to Valerius of Hippo, whom he succeeded in 396. Augustine's theology was formulated in the course of his struggle with three heresies: Manicheism, Donatism, and Pelagianism. His writings are voluminous and his influence on subsequent theology immense. He molded the thought of the Middle Ages down to the thirteenth century. Yet he was above all a pastor and a great spiritual writer.

Twenty-Eighth Sunday in Ordinary Time

Gospel: Luke 17:11-19

It seems that no one has returned to give thanks to God except this stranger.

Commentary: Bruno of Segni

O*n the way to Jerusalem Jesus passed along the border between Samaria and Galilee, and when he entered one of the villages ten lepers came to meet him.* What do these ten lepers stand for if not the sum total of all sinners? When Christ the Lord came not all men and women were leprous in body, but in soul they were, and to have a soul full of leprosy is much worse than to have a leprous body.

But let us see what happened next. *Standing a long way off they called out to him: "Jesus, Master, take pity on us."* They stood a long way off because no one in their condition dared come too close. We stand a long way off too while we continue to sin. To be restored to health and cured of the leprosy of sin, we also must cry out: *Jesus, master, take pity on us.* That cry, however, must come not from our lips but from our heart, for the cry of the heart is louder: it pierces the heavens, rising up to the very throne of God.

When Jesus saw the lepers he told them to go and show themselves to the priests. God has only to look at people to be filled with compassion. He pitied these lepers as soon as he saw them, and sent them to the priests not to be cleansed by them, but to be pronounced clean.

And as they went they were cleansed. Let all sinners listen to this and try to understand it. It is easy for the Lord to forgive sins. Sinners have often been forgiven before they came to a priest. In fact, their repentance and healing occur simultaneously: at the very moment of their conversion they pass from death to life. Let them understand, however, what this conversion means; let them heed the Lord's words:

124

Return to me with all your heart, with fasting, weeping, and mourning; and rend your hearts and not your garments. To be really converted one must be converted inwardly, in one's heart, for *a humbled, contrite heart God will not spurn.*

One of them, when he saw that he was cured, went back again, praising God at the top of his voice. He threw himself at Jesus' feet and thanked him. Now this man was a Samaritan. He stands for all those who, after their cleansing by the waters of baptism or healing by the sacrament of penance, renounce the devil and take Christ as their model, following him with praise, adoration, and thanksgiving, and nevermore abandoning his service.

And Jesus said to him: Stand up and go on your way. Your faith has saved you. Great, therefore, is the power of faith. Without it, as the apostle says, *it is impossible to please God. Abraham believed God and because of this God regarded him as righteous.* Faith saves, faith justifies, faith heals both body and soul.

(On Luke's Gospel 2, 40: PL 165, 426-428)

Bruno of Segni (d.1123) was born near Asti in Piedmont, and studied at the university of Bologna before being made a canon of Siena. At the Council of Rome (1079) he defended the Catholic doctrine of the eucharist against Berengarius. In the following year Gregory VII, his personal friend, made him bishop of Segni, but he refused a cardinalate. Bruno was a zealous pastor, and shared in all the projects of Gregory VII for the reform of the Church. In his writings he attacked simony and lay investiture. He was the greatest scripture commentator of his age. Longing for solitude, he received the monastic habit at Monte Cassino and in 1107 became abbot, but was later ordered by Pope Paschal II to return to his see.

Twenty-Ninth Sunday
in Ordinary Time

Gospel: Luke 18:1-8

God will see those who cry to him vindicated.

Commentary: Gregory of Nyssa

The divine Word teaches us how to pray, explaining to disciples worthy of him, and eagerly longing for knowledge of prayer, what words to use to gain a hearing from God.

Those who fail to unite themselves to God through prayer cut themselves off from God, so the first thing we have to learn from the Word is that we *need to pray continually and not lose heart.* Prayer brings us close to God, and when we are close to God we are far from the Enemy. Prayer safeguards chastity, controls anger, and restrains arrogance. It is the seal of virginity, the assurance of marital fidelity, the shield of travelers, the protection of sleepers, the encouragement of those who keep vigil, the cause of the farmer's good harvest and of the sailor's safety. Therefore I think that even if we spent the whole of our lives in communion with God through thanksgiving and prayer, we should still be as far from adequately repaying our benefactor as we should have been had we not even desired to repay him.

Time has three divisions: past, present, and future. In all three we experience the Lord's kindly healings with us. If you consider the present, you live in him; if you consider the future, your hope of obtaining what you look forward to is in him; if you consider the past, you would not have existed had you not been created by him. Your birth is his kindly gift to you, and after birth his kindness toward you continued, since as the apostle says you live and move in him. On this same kindness depend all your hopes for the future. Only over the present have you any control. Therefore, even if you give thanks to God unceasingly throughout your life you will hardly meet the measure of your debt for present blessings, and as for those of the past and future, you will never find a way of repaying what you owe.

And yet we, who are so far from being capable of showing due gratitude, do not even give thanks to the best of our ability. We fail to set aside, I say not the whole day, but even the smallest portion of the day, to be spent with God.

Who restored to its original beauty that divine image in me that was blurred by sin? Who draws me back to the blessedness I knew before I was driven out of paradise, deprived of the tree of life, and submerged in the abyss of worldliness? As scripture says, *There is no one who understands.* If we realize these things we would give thanks continually, endlessly, throughout the whole of our lives.

(On the Lord's Prayer: PG 44, 1119.1123-1126)

Gregory of Nyssa (c.330-395), the younger brother of Basil the Great, chose a secular career and married. Reluctantly, however, in 371, he received episcopal ordination and became bishop of Nyssa, an unimportant town in Basil's metropolitan district of Caesarea. Gregory was the greatest speculative theologian of the three Cappadocian Fathers, and the first after Origen to attempt a systematic presentation of the Christian faith. Gifted spiritually as well as intellectually, he has been called "the father of Christian mysticism." His spiritual interpretation of scripture shows the influence of Origen.

Thirtieth Sunday
in Ordinary Time

Gospel: Luke 18:9-14

The publican returned home justified; the Pharisee did not.

Commentary: Gregory Palamas

The spiritual champion of evil is full of resources for its furtherance. It has often happened that as soon as the foundations of virtue have been laid in a soul, he has begun to undermine them with despair and lack of faith. Often, too, when the walls of the house of virtue were being built, he has assaulted them by means of inertia and indolence. Even when the house has been roofed over with good works, he has used arrogance and presumption to destroy it.

Nevertheless, stand firm and do not be afraid, for anyone zealous in doing good is even more resourceful. In resisting evil, virtue has the greater power, since it receives heavenly assistance from him who can do all things, and who confirms all virtue's lovers in goodness. Consequently, virtue not only remains unmoved by the manifold wicked wiles of the adversary, but even has the power to raise up and restore those sunk in the depths of evil, and easily to lead them back to God through repentance and humility.

The present parable is sufficient proof; for the tax collector, in spite of his profession and of having lived in the depths of sin, joins the ranks of those living upright lives through a single prayer, and that a short one; he is relieved of his burden of sin, he is lifted up, he rises above all evil, and is admitted to the company of the righteous, justified by the impartial Judge himself. The Pharisee, on the other hand, is condemned by his prayer in spite of being a Pharisee, and in his own eyes a person of importance. Because his "righteousness" is false and his insolence extreme, every syllable he utters provokes God's anger.

But why does humility raise us to the heights of holiness, and self-conceit plunge us into the abyss of sin? It is because when we have a high regard for ourselves, and that in the presence of God, he quite reasonably abandons us, since we think we have no need of his assistance. But when we regard ourselves as nothing and therefore look to heaven for mercy, it is not unreasonable that we should obtain God's compassion, help, and grace. For as Scripture says: *The Lord resists the proud, but gives grace to the humble.*

This man went away justified, and not the other, says the Lord; *because all who exalt themselves will be humbled, but those who humble themselves will be exalted.* For since the devil is pride itself, and arrogance his own particular vice, this sin conquers and drags down with itself every human virtue tinged with it. Similarly, humility before God is the virtue of the good angels, and it conquers every human vice to which a sinner has fallen prey.

Humility is the chariot in which the ascent to God is made upon the clouds that are to carry up to him those destined to be with God for endless ages, according to the apostle's prophecy: *We shall be caught up in the clouds to meet the Lord in the air, and so shall we be always with the Lord.* For humility is like a cloud. Produced by repentance, it draws streams of tears from the eyes, makes unworthy people worthy, and raises up and presents to God those freely justified by reason of their right dispositions.

(Homily 2: PG 151, 17-20.28-29)

Gregory Palamas (1296-1359) was born at Constantinople, and prepared by the piety of his parents for a monastic vocation. At the age of about 20 he became a monk of Mount Athos. In 1347 he was made bishop of Thessalonica. Gregory stressed the biblical teaching that the human body and soul form a single united whole. On this basis he defended the physical exercises used by the Hesychasts in prayer, although he saw these only as a means to an end for those who found them helpful. He followed Saint Basil the Great and Saint Gregory of Nyssa in teaching that although no created intelligence can ever comprehend God in his essence, he can be directly experienced through his uncreated "energies," through which he manifests himself to and is present in the world. God's substance and his energies are distinct from one another, but they are also inseparable. One of these energies is the uncreated divine light, which was seen by the apostles on Mount Tabor. At times this is an inward illumination; at other times it is outwardly manifested.

Thirty-First Sunday in Ordinary Time

Gospel: Luke 19:1-10

The Son of Man came to seek and to find that which was lost.

Commentary: Philoxenus of Mabbug

All who were called by the Lord obeyed his summons at once, provided love of earthly things did not weigh them down. For worldly ties are a weight upon the mind and understanding, and for those bound by them it is difficult to hear the sound of God's call.

But the apostles, and the righteous people and patriarchs before them, were not like this. They obeyed like people really alive, and set out lightly, because no worldly possessions held them bound as though by heavy fetters. Nothing can bind or impede the soul that senses God: it is open and ready, so that the light of the divine voice, each time it comes, finds the soul capable of receiving it.

Our Lord also called Zacchaeus from the sycamore he had climbed, and immediately Zacchaeus hastened to come down, and welcome his disciple even before he was called. And that is a marvelous thing—our Lord had not spoken to him, and Zacchaeus had not seen the Lord with the eyes of the body, and yet he believed in him simply on the word of others. This was because in him faith had been preserved in its natural life and health. He showed his faith by believing in our Lord as soon as he heard he was coming; and the simplicity of his faith was seen when he promised to give half his goods to the poor, and to restore fourfold what he had taken by fraud. For if Zacchaeus' spirit had not been filled at that moment with the simplicity proper to faith, he would not have made this promise to Jesus, and he would not have given out and distributed, in a brief space of time, what his labors had amassed over many years. Simplicity scattered on all sides what had been accumulated by cunning; purity of soul dispersed what had been obtained by guile; faith made a public renunciation of what had been found and appropriated by unrighteousness.

For faith's only possession is God, and it refuses to own anything else besides him. Faith sets no store by possessions of any kind, apart from God, its one lasting possession. Faith has been implanted in us so that we may find God and possess nothing but him, and so that we may recognize that everything that exists is harmful to us apart from him.

(Homily 4, 78: SC 44, 96-97)

Philoxenus (c.440-523), anti-Chalcedonian bishop of Mabbug (Hieropolis), was an outstanding theologian and master of the spiritual life, who achieved a remarkable synthesis between the Syriac and Greek traditions. He was exiled to Thrasia several years before his death. His extensive writings include thirteen orations on the Christian life, five treatises on the Trinity and Incarnation, and several letters. His name is preserved in "Philoxeniana," a Syriac translation of the Bible.

Thirty-Second Sunday in Ordinary Time

Gospel: Luke 20:27-38

He is God, not of the dead, but of the living.

Commentary: John Henry Newman

God spoke to Moses in the burning bush, and called himself the *God of Abraham;* and Christ tells us that in this simple announcement was contained the promise that Abraham should rise again from the dead. In truth, if we may say it with reverence, the all-wise, all-knowing God cannot speak without meaning many things at once. He sees the end from the beginning; he understands the numberless connections and relations of all things one with another. Look at Christ's words, and this same character of them will strike you; whatever he says is fruitful in meaning, and refers to many things. It is well to keep this in mind when we read scripture.

When God called himself the God of Abraham, Isaac, and Jacob, He implied that those holy patriarchs were still alive, though they were no more seen on earth. This may seem evident at first sight; but it may be asked how the text proves that their *bodies* would live; for, if their *souls* were still living, that would be enough to account for their being still called in the Book of Exodus servants of God. Our Blessed Lord seems to tell us, that in some sense or other Abraham's *body* might be considered still alive as a pledge of his resurrection, though it was dead in the common sense in which we apply the word. His announcement is, Abraham *shall* rise from the dead, because in truth he *is* still alive. He cannot in the end be held under the power of the grave, any more than a sleeping man can be kept from waking. Abraham is still alive in the dust, though not risen thence. He is alive because all God's saints live to him, though they seem to perish.

We are apt to talk about our bodies as if we knew how or what they really were; whereas we only know what our eyes tell us. They seem to grow, to come to maturity, to decay; but after all we know no more about them than meets our senses. We have no direct cognizance of what may be called the substantive existence of the body, only of its accidents. Again, we are apt to speak of *soul and body,* and if we could distinguish between them, and knew much about them; but for the most part we use words without meaning. It is useful to make the distinction, and scripture makes it; but after all the gospel speaks of our nature, in a religious sense, *as one.* Soul and body make up one man, which is born once and never dies. Philosophers of old time thought the soul indeed might live for ever, but that the body perished at death; but Christ tells us otherwise, He tells us the body will live for ever. In the text he seems to intimate that it never really dies; that we lose sight indeed of what *we* are accustomed to see, but that God still sees the elements of it which are not exposed to our senses.

God graciously called himself *the God of Abraham.* He did not say the God of Abraham's soul, but simply of "Abraham." He blest Abraham, and he gave him eternal life; not to his soul only, without his body, but to Abraham as one man.

(Parochial and Plain Sermons, Volume 1, pages 271-273)

Newman, John Henry (1801-1890) was born in London and brought up in the Church of England. He went up to Trinity College, Oxford in 1817, became a Fellow of Oriel five years later, was ordained deacon in 1824 and appointed Vicar of Saint Mary's, Oxford, in 1832. The impact of his sermons was tremendous. He was the leading spirit in the Tractarian Movement (1833-1841) and the condemnation of "Tract 90" led to his resignation from Saint Mary's in 1843. Two years later he was received into the Catholic Church. He was ordained in Rome and founded a house of Oratorians in Birmingham. Newman's *Essay on the Development Christian Doctrine* throws light on his withdrawal of previous objections to Roman Catholicism; his *Apologia* reveals the deepest motives underlying his outward attitudes, and the *Grammar of Assent* clarifies the subjective content of commitment to faith. In 1879 he was made a cardinal and he died at Edgbaston in 1890.

Thirty-Third Sunday
in Ordinary Time

Gospel: Luke 21:5-19

Your endurance will win you your life.

Commentary: Nilus of Ancyra

In time of trial it is of great profit to us patiently to endure for God's sake, for the Lord says: *By patient endurance you will win life for yourselves.* He did not say by your fasting, or your solitude and silence, or your singing of psalms, although all of these are helpful in saving your soul. But he said: *By patient endurance* in every trial that overtakes you, and in every affliction, whether this be insolent and contemptuous treatment, or any kind of disgrace, either small or great; whether it be bodily weakness, or the belligerent attacks of Satan, or any trial whatsoever caused either by other people or by evil spirits.

By patient endurance you will win life for yourselves, although to this must be added wholehearted thanksgiving, and prayer, and humility. For you must be ready to bless and praise your benefactor, God the Savior of the world, who disposes all things, good or otherwise, for your benefit.

The apostle writes: *With patient endurance we run the race of faith set before us.* For what has more power than virtue? What more firmness or strength than patient endurance? Endurance, that is, for God's sake. This is the queen of virtues, the foundation of virtue, a haven of tranquility. It is peace in time of war, calm in rough waters, safety amidst treachery and danger. It makes those who practice it stronger than steel. No weapons or brandished bows, no turbulent troops or advancing siege engines, no flying spears or arrows can shake it. Not even the host of evil spirits, nor the dark array of hostile powers, nor the devil himself standing by with all his armies and devices will have power to injure the man or woman who has acquired this virtue through Christ.

(Letters III, 35: PG 79, 401-404)

Nilus (+c.430), a native of Ancyra, studied at Constantinople where he became a disciple of Saint John Chrysostom. He afterwards founded a monastery near Ancyra where he exercised a wide influence, partly by correspondence: he is known to have written at least 1,061 letters. His writings include treatises on the preeminence of monks, monastic observance, and voluntary poverty.

Christ the King
Thirty-Fourth Sunday in Ordinary Time

Gospel: Luke 23:35-43

Lord, remember me when you come into your kingdom.

Commentary: Bernard of Clairvaux

The Lord God will give him the throne of his father David. These are the angel's words to the Virgin concerning the son he had announced, promising that he should succeed to the kingdom of David. No one questions the origin of our Lord Jesus from the line of David, but how, I wonder, will God give him the throne of David, since Jesus never reigned in Jerusalem and would not consent to the crowds who would make him king—he even protested before Pilate that his kingdom was not of this world. Besides, what importance could be attached to his sitting on the throne of David his father when he was already seated on the cherubim, on a throne high and lifted up, as the prophet says? But we know that another Jerusalem is meant, different from the present one where David once reigned, a city much nobler and richer. God will indeed give him the throne of his father David when he has established him as king over Zion, his holy mountain—he will give him not a symbolic but a real throne, not a temporal but an eternal throne, not an earthly but a heavenly throne.

He shall reign over the house of Jacob for ever, and of his kingdom there shall be no end. Again, if we take this in a temporal sense, how is it that Christ will reign for ever over something not eternal in itself? We must look, then, for a house of Jacob that is eternal, over which he will reign for ever. Are there any among us who, in accordance with the meaning of the name Jacob (supplanter), will supplant the devil in their hearts, struggle against their vices and desires, so that sin will not reign in their bodies, but Jesus only, through grace now, through glory for all eternity? Blessed are they in whom Jesus will reign for ever, for they shall reign with him, and of his kingdom there shall be no end. Oh how glorious is that kingdom where kings are gathered together to give united praise and honor to the King of kings and Lord of lords, in the contemplation of whose splendor the just shall shine like the sun in the kingdom of their Father. Oh that Jesus, out of the love he has for his people, may remember me, a sinner, when he comes into his kingdom! Oh that he may deign to come and save me on the day when he delivers up his kingdom to his God and Father, so that I may see the joy of his chosen ones and rejoice in the gladness of his people. Then I too shall be able to praise him together with his inheritance.

And now, Lord Jesus, come and remove the stumbling-blocks within the kingdom which is my soul, so that you who ought to may reign in it. Greed comes along and claims its throne in me; arrogance would dominate me; pride would be my king. Comfort and pleasure say: We shall reign! Ambition, detraction, envy, anger fight within me for supremacy, and seem to have me entirely in their power. But I resist insofar as I can; I struggle against them insofar as I receive your help. I protest that Jesus is my Lord. I keep myself for him since I acknowledge his rights over me. To me he is God, to me he is the Lord, and I declare: I will have no king but the Lord Jesus! Come then, Lord, rout them by your power and you will reign in me, for you are my king and my God, who grant victories to Jacob.

(Hom. IV super Missus est, 1-2: PL 183, 78-80)

Bernard (1090-1153) entered the monastery of Citeaux with thirty companions in 1112. He received his monastic training under the abbot, Saint Stephen Harding, who sent him in 1115 to make a foundation at Clairvaux in France. Soon one of the most infuential religious forces in Europe, Bernard was instrumental in founding the Knights Templar and in the election of Pope Innocent I in 1130. He was a strenuous opponent of writers such as Aberlard, Gilbert de la Porrée, and Henry of Lausanne. Above all, Bernard was a monk; his sermons and theological writings show an intimate knowledge of scripture, a fine eloquence, and an extraordinarily sublime mysticism.

Presentation of the Lord

Gospel: Luke 2:22-40 or 22-32

My eyes have seen your saving power.

Commentary: Guerric of Igny

As today we hold our burning candles, who could fail immediately to recall that venerable old man who, on this day, took Jesus in his arms, the Word who was latent in a body as light is in wax, and declared him to be the light to enlighten the nations? Indeed, Simeon himself was also a bright and shining lamp, which bore witness to the light. He came to the temple under the influence of the Spirit which filled him precisely in order that, receiving your loving-kindness, O God, in the midst of your temple, he might proclaim Jesus as that loving-kindness and the light of your people.

There, then, is the candle alight in Simeon's hands: do you light your own candles by enkindling them at his—those lamps which the Lord commanded you to have in your hands. Come to him and be enlightened so that you do not so much carry lamps as become them, shining within and without for yourselves and for your neighbors. So may there be a lamp in your heart, in your hand and in your mouth: let the lamp in your heart shine for yourself, the lamp in your hand and mouth for your neighbors. The lamp in your heart is faith-inspired reverence, the lamp in your hand the example of good works, the lamp in your mouth edifying speech. We have to shine not only before other people by our good works and by what we say, but also before the angels by prayer and before God by our purpose. In the presence of the angels our lamp is reverence without alloy when we sing attentively in their sight or pray fervently; before God our lamp is a single-minded resolve to please him alone to whom we have commended ourselves.

138

In order to light all these lamps for yourselves, approach the source of light and become enlightened—I mean Jesus who shines in Simeon's hands to light up your faith, shine on your works, inspire your speech, make your prayer fervent and refine your intentions. Then when the lamp of this life goes out, there will appear for you who had so many lamps shining within you the light of unquenchable life, and it will shine for you at evening like the brightness of midday. Though you may have thought yourself completely used up, you will rise like the daystar and your darkness will be as bright as noon. No longer will you need the sun to shine for you by day nor will the brightness of the moon give you light; instead the Lord will be an everlasting light for you because the luminary of the new Jerusalem is the Lamb. To him be praise and splendor for ever. Amen.

(The Feast of the Purification, Sermon 1, 2.3.5: PL 185, 64-67)

Guerric of Igny (c.1070/1080-1157), about whose early life little is known, probably received his education at the cathedral school of Tournai, perhaps under the influence of Odo of Cambrai (1807-1092). He seems to have lived a retired life of prayer and study near the cathedral of Tournai. He paid a visit to Clairvaux to consult Saint Bernard, and is mentioned by him as a novice in a letter to Ogerius in 1125/1256. He became abbot of the Cistercian abbey of Igny, in the diocese of Rheims in 1138. A collection of 54 authentic sermons preached on Sundays and feast days has been edited. Guerric's spirituality was influenced by Origen.

Birth of Saint John the Baptist

Gospel: Luke 1:57-66.80

John is his name.

Commentary: Rabanus Maurus

Today we celebrate the physical birth of Saint John the Baptist. Our Lord's birth and Saint John's are rightly celebrated throughout the world, because each is a great mystery. A barren woman gave birth to John, a virgin conceived Christ; barrenness was overcome in Elizabeth, the normal manner of conception was changed in blessed Mary. It was through knowing her husband that Elizabeth brought forth a son: Mary believed the angel and conceived a man. Elizabeth conceived a man who was only a man: Mary conceived both God and man.

Great then is John. The Savior bore witness to his greatness when he said *among those born of women there has arisen no one greater than John the Baptist.* He excels all, every single person; he surpasses the prophets, he is superior to the patriarchs. Everyone born of woman is inferior to John, but the son of the Virgin is greater than he, as John himself said: *He who comes after me ranks before me, and I am not worthy to undo his sandal strap.*

In the birth of our Lord's forerunner and in our Redeemer's birth there is this mystery: the prophet's birth signifies our humility, but the Lord's our exaltation. John was born as the days began to grow shorter: Christ as they grew longer, because it was fitting that man's reputation should decrease and God's glory increase. John realized this when he said: *I must decrease and he must increase.* John was sent ahead like a voice before a word, a lamp before the sun, a crier before a judge, a servant before his master, the best man before the bridegroom.

We have recognized the blessed forerunner of the Lord as a lamp which went ahead of the true light and gave witness to the light so that everyone might believe through him, so let us have recourse to him and listen to his urgent message. He indeed is the voice spoken of by the prophet Isaiah, *the voice of one calling in the wilderness: Prepare the way of the Lord, make his paths straight. Every valley shall be filled, and every mountain and hill made low, the crooked shall be made straight and the rough ways smooth, and all humankind shall see the salvation of God.* Let us, too, prepare a way for the Lord who is to come into our hearts; let us remove the obstacles of sin by confession and repentance, straighten the paths of our life which hitherto have been so wayward and devious; let us pave the way of true faith with good works, get rid of worldly arrogance, and lift up our faint hearts. When everything has been arranged, put in order, smoothed, and reunited we shall see God's salvation as he is, for *his place is in peace and his abode in Zion.*

May he, Jesus Christ our Savior, through the prayers of his forerunner, grant us to enjoy for all eternity the vision of him who for this reason came down from heaven and, triumphing over death, ascended on high where he lives and reigns with the Father and the Holy Spirit, God for ever and ever. Amen.

(Homilies on Special Feasts XXVI: PL 110, 51-52)

Rabanus Maurus (776/784-856) entered the monastery of Fulda, and was sent from there to Tours to study under Alcuin. On his return he was made master of the monastic school at Fulda, which became under him one of the most influential in Europe. Maurus was ordained priest in 814 and elected abbot in 822. In 842 he resigned and led a life of prayer and study at Petersburg, near Fulda, until his election as archbishop of Mainz in 847. As abbot and as archbishop he did much to further the evangelization of Germany. He was one of the greatest theologians of his age, and his zeal for learning won him the title, "Teacher of Germany."

Saints Peter and Paul

Gospel: Matthew 16:13-19

You are Peter, and I will give you the keys of the kingdom of heaven.

Commentary: Peter of Blois

"I saw men united, and an angel of the Lord spoke, saying: These are holy men who have become friends of God."

Who are these men who are united? Surely they are the venerable princes of the earth and of the Church, Peter and Paul. The same faith united them; the same city, the same way of life, the same day made them equal in martyrdom under the same tyrant. Since then they have been united in so many ways, it is right that they share the same feast.

Christ changed Saul into Paul, and Simon into Peter: for it is of these that the prophet had once foretold: *And he will call his servants by a new name. You are Peter,* Christ said, *and on this rock I will build my church. The rock was Christ,* and Christ gave Peter his own name, so that Peter might be a rock. For as, in the desert, water flowed from the rock for the thirsty people, so too there flowed from Peter a saving confession of faith for others who were thirsty for faith.

When Christ was about to ascend to heaven, he entrusted to Peter the feeding of his sheep and lambs. Peter had been used to steering a small boat, but now Christ put him at the helm of a great ship: he made him head of the whole Church. To Peter, as the best steward, he handed over the keys of his house. Peter's righteousness made him such a powerful judge that the judgment of heaven depends on his decision; not even an angel would presume to challenge his sentence.

When the Lord asked him who people were saying he was, in a brief confession of faith Peter proclaimed the mystery of the divine majesty in Christ. It was not flesh and blood that revealed this to you, Peter (for it is not flesh and blood that will possess the kingdom of God), but the Spirit of God the Father, who is in heaven. The admirable fisherman, who once searched the depths of the sea, faithfully confessed the inscrutable mystery of the godhead in Christ. In answer to the Lord's question: "Peter, do you love me?" Peter blotted out his triple denial with a triple confession of faith.

Peter fell, Paul was thrown to the ground; both were made weak that they might rise again strong and perfect. When Peter relied on his own strength, the intrepidity of his promise to stand firm was matched by the gravity of his fall. Yet after that detestable sin of apostasy, Peter obtained the highest place among the teachers of the faith and in the Church. Paul, who was struck blind and thrown to the ground, was raised to the third heaven to contemplate, with purified mental eye, the heavenly court's inexpressible glory.

I believe that by remembering the glorious death of these two, we honor all the apostles and martyrs; for we venerate them as martyrs and as the most outstanding of the apostles. How blessed is the martyrdom, how glorious the death that makes those who die with Christ immortal, so that united with him in a death like his they now reign with him! *To the eyes of the foolish they appeared to die, and their death was thought an affliction;* but *blessed are those who die in the Lord.* They fell asleep in Christ to become co-heirs with Christ.

(Sermon 28: PL 207, 644-646)

Peter of Blois (1135-1212) was born at Blois, near Tours, and like many of his contemporaries he studied at the schools of Tours, Bologna, and Paris. About 1175 he became archdeacon of Bath. Later he served as secretary to Archbishops Richard and Baldwin of Canterbury. He became archdeacon of London about 1202 and was ordained priest.

Transfiguration of the Lord

Gospel: Luke 9:28-36

As he was praying, his face was transformed.

Commentary: Gregory Palamas

The Savior took with him just Peter, James, and John and led them up a high mountain where, before their eyes, he was transfigured. What does "He was transfigured" mean? asks the golden-mouthed theologian. It means that it was his good pleasure to give them a small glimpse of his divine nature. He let the disciples see God dwelling within him.

Saint Luke says that as he was praying the appearance of his face changed. Matthew writes that it shone like the sun. But he did not say that it was like the sun to make us think of that light as of something perceptible to the senses, but rather to teach us that what the sun is to those who live on the level of sense perception and whose vision is limited by sense perception, that Christ in his divine nature is to those who live by the Spirit and see in the Spirit; nor do those who are like God need any other light by which to see God. Those who enjoy eternal life have no other light but him: why should they want another light when they have the greatest?

It was in prayer that he shone like this in the company of the preeminent prophets, revealing in some indescribable way that indescribable light to his chosen disciples, to show that that blessed vision was the fruit of prayer, and to teach us that drawing near to God by virtue and mental union with him is what causes this radiance to appear. It is given to all and seen by all who by pure prayer and the conscientious performance of good works continually reach out to God.

Chrysostom says that the true beauty, the most exquisite beauty of the blessed Godhead is to be seen only by those whose minds have been purified. By gazing at its dazzling beauty they receive some share in it, some bright beam as it were that lights up their own faces. Thus the face of Moses too became resplendent when he talked with God. Do you not remember how he too was transfigured when he went up the mountain, and so saw the glory of the Lord? But his transfiguration came not from himself but from Another, whereas our Lord Jesus Christ possessed that splendor by nature. He had therefore no need of prayer to make his body shine with divine light, but he prayed to show what would enable the saints to receive and behold the divine splendor. For *the righteous* too *will shine like the sun in the kingdom of their Father.* And so, having become all divine light, as children of divine light they will see Christ in his unspeakable and divine splendor, the splendor proceeding naturally from his divinity, in which his body shared because of his unity of person, as was shown on Mount Tabor. Such was the light that made his face shine like the sun.

(Homily 34: PG 151, 429-432)

Gregory Palamas (1296-1359) was born at Constantinople, and prepared by the piety of his parents for a monastic vocation. At the age of about 20 he became a monk of Mount Athos. In 1347 he was made bishop of Thessalonica. Gregory stressed the biblical teaching that the human body and soul form a single united whole. On this basis he defended the physical exercises used by the Hesychasts in prayer, although he saw these only as a means to an end for those who found them helpful. He followed Saint Basil the Great and Saint Gregory of Nyssa in teaching that although no created intelligence can ever comprehend God in his essence, he can be directly experienced through his uncreated "energies," through which he manifests himself to and is present in the world. God's substance and his energies are distinct from one another, but they are also inseparable. One of these energies is the uncreated divine light, which was seen by the apostles on Mount Tabor. At times this is an inward illumination; at other times it is outwardly manifested.

Assumption of the Blessed Virgin Mary

Gospel: Luke 1:39-56

The Mighty One has done great things to me and has exalted the humble.

Commentary: Nicolas Cabasilas

It was fitting that the Virgin should share in every aspect of her Son's providential care for us. Just as she had bestowed her flesh and blood on him and had received a share of his graces in return, so in like manner she also participated in all his pains and sufferings. When his side was wounded by the lance as he hung on the cross a sword pierced his Mother's heart, as saintly Simeon had foretold. And so, after our Savior's death, she was the first to conform herself to the Son who resembled her, and hence she shared in his resurrection before all others.

When her Son had broken the tyranny of death by rising from the grave, the Virgin saw him and heard his salutation; and when the time came for him to depart for heaven, she escorted him on his way, as far as she could. Finally, when he had gone away, she took his place among the apostles, uniting herself with the other companions of our Savior by means of her good works, through which she benefitted the whole human race. She more truly than anyone else made up what was lacking in Christ; for who could more fittingly do so than his Mother?

Now it was necessary for her most holy soul to be separated from her hallowed body; and it was indeed released and united with the soul of her Son, the second light with the first. For a short time her body remained upon earth and then it too departed. It had to go everywhere the Savior had gone, and to shed its light on both the living and the dead. It had to sanctify nature in every respect; then, at last, it could take its appointed place. And so the grave received it for a short time, but heaven soon took from the grave that new earth, that spiritual body, that treasury of our life, more revered than the angels, holier than the archangels. His throne was restored to the King, paradise to the tree of life, the sun's orb to the light, the tree to its fruit, the Mother to her Son; for in every respect she was in accord with her Child.

O blessed one, what words can adequately praise your virtue, or the graces you received from our Savior for the benefit of the whole human race? It would be impossible to do so even if one could speak in the tongues of humans and of angels, to use the words of Paul. It seems to me that part of the eternal happiness in store for the righteous will be really to know and proclaim your graces in a fitting way. For these *no eye has seen nor ear heard.* To use the noble John's words: *The world cannot contain them.* The only theater in which your marvelous gifts can fittingly be displayed is the new heaven and the new earth where the sun is the sun of Righteousness whom darkness neither precedes nor follows. The Savior himself will proclaim your worth, and the angels will applaud.

(Marian Homilies: PO 19 [1926] 508-509)

Nicolas Cabasilas (b.1322/23) was a native of Thessalonica. After receiving an excellent education, first at Thessalonica and then in Constantinople, he entered the imperial service, in which for ten years he played a prominent part. After the deposition in 1354 of his friend, the emperor John VI Cantacuzenos, Cabasilas entered the Manganon monastery near Constantinople, and probably became a priest. This was the period of his greatest literary output, his two principal works being *The Life in Christ* and *A Commentary on the Divine Liturgy,* both of which were written for lay people. The kernel of Cabasilas' teaching, which was praised by the Council of Trent and by Bossuet, is the Christians' deification by means of the sacraments. Cabasilas died some time after the capture of Thessalonica by the Turks in 1387.

Triumph of the Cross

Gospel: John 3:13-17

The Son of Man must be lifted up.

Commentary: Gregory of Nyssa

With regard to the cross, the following is the teaching which tradition has handed down to us.

In the gospel all words and actions have a higher, more divine meaning. There is no exception to this rule: there is nothing that does not reveal itself as in every way a mixture of the divine and the human. The utterance or the action proceeds in human fashion, while the mystical meaning reveals the divine element. It follows, then, that with regard to the cross also we should not notice the one aspect and overlook the other. We should see the human element in the death, but try to penetrate the divine significance in the way it occurred.

Now it belongs to the Godhead to pervade all things and to extend throughout every part of the substance of whatever exists. For nothing can remain in being without remaining in him who exists, and that which exists in the proper and primary sense is the Divine Nature. The permanence of existing things therefore compels us to believe that this Nature pervades everything. We learn this from the shape of the cross, since it is divided into four parts in such a way that the four arms converge in the middle; for he who was stretched upon it when God's plan was fulfilled by his death is the one who binds all things to himself and makes them one. In his own person he brings the diverse natures of existing things into one accord and harmony. For we conceive of things as either above or below, or we may think of them as extended sideways. If, then, you consider the constitution of things in heaven or under the earth or at either extremity of the universe, everywhere your thought is met in advance by the Godhead, who alone is perceived to be in every part of existing things, and who maintains all things in being.

Since, then, the whole creation looks to God, has its center in him, and through him acquires cohesion, things above being through him united to those below and things at one end with those at the other, it was fitting that knowledge of God should come to us not only through hearing, but that sight also should be our teacher in these sublime matters. This was the starting point even of the great Paul when he initiated the people of Ephesus into the Christian mysteries, and by his teaching implanted in them the power to know *what is the depth and the height, and the breadth and the length.* He designates each projection of the cross by its own proper term, speaking of the upper part as height, and the lower part as depth, and the extension on either side as breadth and length. I think he brings out this idea still more clearly in his letter to the Philippians when he says: *At the name of Jesus Christ all beings in heaven, on earth, and in the underworld shall bend the knee.* There he refers to the central cross-beam by a single term, *on earth,* designating everything that lies between the heavenly beings and those in the underworld.

This is the mystical meaning we have been taught with regard to the cross.

(*Srawley, CPT, pages 117-121*)

Gregory of Nyssa (c.330-395), the younger brother of Basil the Great, chose a secular career and married. Reluctantly, however, in 371, he received episcopal ordination and became bishop of Nyssa, an unimportant town in Basil's metropolitan district of Caesarea. Gregory was the greatest speculative theologian of the three Cappadocian Fathers, and the first after Origen to attempt a systematic presentation of the Christian faith. Gifted spiritually as well as intellectually, he has been called "the father of Christian mysticism." His spiritual interpretation of scripture shows the influence of Origen.

All Saints

Gospel: Matthew 5:1-12

Be glad and rejoice, for your reward will be great in heaven.

Commentary: Anastasius of Sinai

How can we explain our zeal in attending this solemn gathering today, beloved, if not by the fact that our brothers and sisters who have been called away from us to Christ have summoned us all here? Gladly then let us come to Christ with songs of praise, for our departed ones have inspired us to glorify God for them on earth, while they join the choirs of angels in praising him in heaven, and provide a spiritual meal for us. Filled with the delights of paradise, they place before us the wine of compunction. They now enjoy the consolations of heaven and are kindling a light to enlighten their own hearts as they move toward the unapproachable Light.

The saints already with Christ have drawn away the saints from among ourselves. Those who were once with us have departed from us, returning to their true homeland and leaving us orphans. They have passed from a state of corruptibility to one of incorruptibility; they have gone from this world and risen again in Christ, exchanging their tent-dwelling for the heavenly Jerusalem. Leaving to us the emptiness of this life, they have attained to the bliss of heaven; leaving to us our earthly worries, they have passed to a land without worry. They have left behind the winds and waves of this world and have anchored in harbors of perfect calm.

Yet even while they seemed to be with us they were not so in reality, for their minds were turned to God. They lived on earth as citizens of heaven. Having here no lasting city, they sought a heavenly one; having no earthly riches, they sought the riches of heaven. They were strangers and sojourners as their ancestors were. Strangers to the world, to the things of the world, and to the ways of the world, their whole heart was absorbed in the things of heaven; these were the things they thought about and were concerned about. They longed for the beauty of heaven, its mansions and dwellings, its choirs and hymnody, its feasts and its eternal blessedness.

The saints contemplated, sought, and hastened toward these things, and so at last they attained them. Their striving was rewarded by admission to the heavenly bridal chamber. Because they labored they now exult. Because they were not negligent they now rejoice. *Precious in the eyes of the Lord is the death of his saints.*

(Sermon: PG 89, 1192-1193)

Anastasius of Sinai (d.599), a Palestinian monk of Sinai, became Patriarch of Antioch in 559. He opposed the decree of Justinian I which ascribed impassability to Christ's human nature, and in 570 was banished to Jerusalem. Five of his works against the heresy have survived in Latin. He was much quoted by later Greek theologians, and because of his close reasoning is considered a precursor of the scholastics. In 593 at the urging of his friend Gregory the Great he was restored to his see, where he was succeeded in due course by another Anastasius, also an author who is considered a martyr. Yet a third Anastasius called Sinaita wrote against the Monophysites in the mid-seventeenth century.

All Souls

Gospel: John 6:37-40

I will raise them up on the last day.

Commentary: Odilo of Cluny

Christians are absolutely certain of the divine promise that the dead will rise again. Truth himself made the promise and Truth cannot lie. The promise given by Truth concerning the resurrection of the dead is reliable because, since Truth cannot lie, he must fulfill all he has promised. Moreover, to give us certain proof that bodies will rise again, the Lord himself deigned to demonstrate this to us in his own body. Christ rose so that Christians may not doubt that they too will rise: for what happened first in the head will happen later in the body.

Now we should realize, beloved, that there are two deaths and two resurrections: scripture speaks of a first death and a second death. The first, moreover, has two parts: in the one the guilty soul forsakes its Creator by sinning; in the other it is, by God's judgment, separated from its body as a penalty. The second death includes the death of the body and the everlasting punishment of the soul. The first death temporarily separates from their bodies the souls of good and bad alike. In the second death the wicked alone suffer torment in both body and soul for ever.

In the past all were subject to both deaths, for original sin made everyone liable to punishment. But the immortal and righteous Son of God came and took mortal flesh from us in order to die for us. In that flesh he bore the punishment for sin, but without any guilt, for there could be no sin in him. God's Son thus accepted on our behalf the second part of the first death, the death of the body alone, and by so doing rescued us from the control of sin and from the torment of everlasting punishment.

Christ now continues his merciful work: to those whom he encourages to live a good life he gives faith so that they may believe correctly, and charity so that they may readily devote themselves to good works. On the last day he will graciously raise them up in the body in order to give them everlasting blessedness. Therefore, beloved, now that our souls have been restored to life by faith, let us live uprightly so that we may rise to everlasting joy in our bodies as well. Let us be aware of the gift Christ has given us in the first resurrection, so that when we rise in the body we may deserve to reign with our Savior for ever. Then death will be swallowed up in victory, and believers will be given true life and true joy. In return for their faith and good works they will receive the kingdom of heaven from their Savior who is God Almighty, and who lives and reigns with the Father and the Holy Spirit through endless ages. Amen.

(Sermon 5 on the Lord's Resurrection: PL 142, 1004-1005)

Odilo (962-1049) entered the monastery of Cluny in 991 and a few years later was elected abbot, a position he held for fifty years. Under his rule the number of Cluniac houses increased from thirty-seven to sixty-five and their influence was widespread. Odilo left a lasting mark on the liturgy by introducing the commemoration of the dead on All Souls' day. From Cluny this observance spread throughout the Western Church. Odilo wrote a number of letters and sermons, most of which treat of the Blessed Virgin and the mysteries of redemption, especially the incarnation.

Dedication
of the Lateran Basilica

Gospel: John 2:13-22

Jesus spoke about the temple of his own body.

Commentary: Augustine of Hippo

G*od's temple is holy, and you are that temple:* all you who believe in Christ and whose belief makes you love him. Real belief in Christ means love of Christ: it is not the belief of the demons who believed without loving and therefore despite their belief said: *What do you want with us, Son of God?* No; let our belief be full of love for him we believe in, so that instead of saying: *What do you want with us,* we may rather say: We belong to you, you have redeemed us. All who believe in this way are like the living stones which go to build God's temple, and like the rot-proof timber used in the framework of the ark which the flood waters could not submerge. It is in this temple, that is, in ourselves, that prayer is addressed to God and heard by him.

But to pray in God's temple we must pray in the peace of the Church, in the unity of the body of Christ, which is made up of many believers throughout the world. When we pray in this temple our prayers are heard, because whoever prays in the peace of the Church prays in spirit and in truth.

Our Lord's driving out of the temple people who were seeking their own ends, who came to the temple to buy and sell, is symbolic. For if that temple was a symbol it obviously follows that the body of Christ, the true temple of which the other was an image, has within it some who are buyers and sellers, or in other words, people who are seeking their own interests and not those of Jesus Christ.

But the temple was not destroyed by the people who wanted to turn the house of God into a den of thieves, and neither will those who live evil lives in the Catholic Church, and do all they can to convert God's house into a robbers' den succeed in destroying the temple. The time will come when they will be driven out by a whip made of their own sins.

This temple of God, this body of Christ, this assembly of believers, has but one voice, and sings the psalms as though it were but one person. If we wish, it is our voice; if we wish, we may listen to the singer with our ears and ourselves sing in our hearts. But if we choose not to do so it will mean that we are like buyers and sellers, preoccupied with our own interests.

(Expositions of the Psalms 130: CCL 40, 1898-1900)

Augustine (354-430) was born at Thagaste in Africa and received a Christian education, although he was not baptized until 387. In 391 he was ordained priest and in 395 he became coadjutor bishop to Valerius of Hippo, whom he succeeded in 396. Augustine's theology was formulated in the course of his struggle with three heresies: Manicheism, Donatism, and Pelagianism. His writings are voluminous and his influence on subsequent theology immense. He molded the thought of the Middle Ages down to the thirteenth century. Yet he was above all a pastor and a great spiritual writer.

Immaculate Conception

Gospel: Luke 1:26-38

Rejoice, most favored one, the Lord is with you.

Commentary: Sophronius of Jerusalem

Hail, full of grace, the Lord is with you. Truly *blessed are you among women,* for you have changed the curse of Eve into a blessing and caused Adam, once accursed, to be blessed through you. Truly *blessed are you among women,* for it was through you that the Father's blessing dawned on humankind and freed it from the ancient curse. Truly *blessed are you among women,* for through you your ancestors will be saved, since you are going to bear the Savior who will gain them God's salvation. Truly *blessed are you among women,* for without seed you produced the fruit that brings blessing to all the earth, releasing it from the curse that made it bear thorns. Truly *blessed are you among women,* for though by nature you are a woman, you will in very truth become the mother of God: if he who is to be born of you is truly God incarnate, then, since you will be giving birth to God, you will with perfect justice be called the mother of God.

Do not be afraid, Mary, for you have found favor with God that can never be lost. You have won from God a most glorious favor, a grace long desired, a grace of great splendor, a saving grace, an unfailing grace, a grace that will last for ever. Many before you have been holy, but no one has been as favored as you, no one as blessed as you, no one as perfectly sanctified as you, no one as highly praised as you. No one else has like you been possessed from the first by purifying grace, no one else has been enlightened like you, or exalted like you, for no one has approached so close to God as you, or been enriched with such divine gifts, or endowed with such heavenly grace.

You surpass all human desire; you surpass all the gifts given by God to the whole human race, for God's dwelling within you has made you richer than all others. No one else has been able to contain God as you do; no one else has been capable of receiving God as you have; no one else has deserved to be so enlightened by God. And therefore you have not only received God, the Creator and Lord of the universe, but he has in an unheard-of way taken flesh from you; you bear him in your womb, and will later give birth to him who will redeem humankind from the Father's sentence, and confer on it eternal salvation.

(Homily 2, 21.22.25: PG 87/3, 3241. 3245-3248)

Sophronius (c.560-c.638) was born in Damascus and became a monk at Jerusalem about 580. In 633 he visited the patriarchs of Alexandria and Constantinople in vain attempts to wean them from the Monothelite heresy. When in the following year he was elected Patriarch of Jerusalem, he convened a synod to promulgate the teaching of Chalcedon, and sent a long and learned synodal letter to the other patriarchs setting out the doctrine of the two natures in Christ. This was praised at the Third Council of Constantinople in 681. He wrote lives of several saints as well as meditations in verse; nine of his sermons survive. He died in the year after the Saracens had captured Jerusalem.

Index of Scripture

Index of Authors